# IMAGES OF WAR

# THE BATTLE OF IWO JIMA

Iwo Jima, February 1945. Marines marching inland from the beach.

# IMAGES OF WAR

# THE BATTLE OF IWO JIMA

*Raising the Flag
February–March 1945*

## RARE PHOTOGRAPHS FROM WARTIME ARCHIVES

## Mark Khan

FRONTLINE
BOOKS

**FRONTLINE
BOOKS**

First published in Great Britain in 2018 by
FRONTLINE BOOKS
an imprint of
Pen & Sword Books Ltd, Yorkshire and Philadelphia

ISBN 978 1 84832 449 7

Typeset in Gill Sans by CHIC GRAPHICS

Printed and bound by CPI Group (UK) Ltd, Croydon, CR0 4YY

Pen & Sword Books Ltd incorporates the imprints of Pen & Sword Aviation, Pen & Sword
Family History, Pen & Sword Maritime, Pen & Sword Military, Pen & Sword Discovery,
Wharncliffe Local History, Wharncliffe True Crime, Wharncliffe Transport, Pen and Sword
Select, Pen and Sword Military Classics, Leo Cooper, The Praetorian Press, Remember
When, Seaforth Publishing and Frontline Publishing and White Owl

*For a complete list of Pen & Sword titles please contact*
PEN & SWORD BOOKS LIMITED
47 Church Street, Barnsley, South Yorkshire, S70 2AS, England
E-mail: enquiries@pen-and-sword.co.uk
Website: www.pen-and-sword.co.uk

PEN & SWORD BOOKS LIMITED
1950 Lawrence Road, Havertown, PA 19083, USA
E-mail: Uspen-and-sword@casematepublishers.com
Website: www.penandswordbooks.com

# Contents

# Introduction

By February 1945 American forces had fought their way across the Pacific in a series of land, air, and sea battles combined with amphibious assaults. The campaign to liberate the Philippines was progressing well. The Southern Mariana Islands of Guam, Saipan and Tinian had been captured in August 1944. It was on Saipan and Tinian that airbases were set up to allow American B-29 heavy bombers to conduct long-range raids against industrial and military targets in the Japanese home islands (approximately 1,500 miles away). The first raids on Japan by Saipan-based B-29 bombers took place on 24 November 1944, and Tinian-based B-29s on 4 February 1945. American forces in the Pacific were now poised to strike deep at the heart of Japan.

The next phase of these operations was to be directed at the small volcanic island of Iwo Jima, located approximately 750 miles to the south of Tokyo and part of a chain of islands known as the Nanpo Shoto. This island chain is formed of three major island groups. From north to south these groups comprise: the Izu shotō, the Ogasawara Guntō (Bonin Islands), and the Kazan Rettō (Volcano Islands). Iwo Jima lies within the latter. It is also often referred to as Sulphur Island. The island was eventually handed back to Japan and is known today as Iōtō (Ioto).

Iwo Jima measures approximately 4 miles along its north-east–south-west axis, with the width varying from about 2½ miles to slightly less than ½ a mile at the narrowest part, which lies at the south-western tip of the island where the dormant volcano Mount Suribachi is located. The landmass of the island covers approximately 8 square miles.

The Japanese had built airfields on the island, which they used to launch raids on American-held islands and against US bombers attacking Japan. The decision to capture Iwo Jima was not only taken to deny the enemy the use of the island as an important defensive base, but also allow US forces to operate the airfield facilities in support of their bombing campaign against the Japanese mainland. Iwo Jima is located approximately 700 miles from the air bases on Saipan and Tinian and lay just off the route of B-29s attacking Japan. Following on from the capture of the island, it was planned that US forces would develop an advanced air base to support offensive air operations against the Japanese mainland. From Iwo Jima US fighter escort squadrons could be used to provide cover over Japan itself; B-29 bombers in trouble or short of fuel could land at Iwo Jima; and offensive operations could be launched from Iwo Jima with increased bomb payloads as less fuel was required due to the closer proximity to Japan than bases farther away.

Aware of the island's strategic value, the Japanese had installed a large garrison and built strong defences, including bunkers, gun positions, anti-invasion defences and a complex system of underground tunnels and caves.

In preparation for the amphibious attack, the island had been subjected to substantial pre-emptive aerial and surface bombardments since June 1944. It was clear to the Japanese defenders that an operation to capture the island was going to happen. It was just a question of when.

From an attacker's perspective, there was no hope of surprise, which was a major disadvantage. The entire operation was going to be fought virtually on the terms of the defenders. It was going to be, in effect, a series of frontal assaults made with little room to manoeuvre against a defender that had spent months preparing to fight a defensive battle to the last man.

An attack on such a strongly fortified position would not normally be undertaken unless it could possibly be avoided. The strategic importance of Iwo Jima meant that these normal considerations had to be overridden. To ensure the best possible chance of taking the island, adequate troops, support, weapons, equipment and supplies were made available. The attacking forces also enjoyed a superiority derived from experience gained in previous amphibious operations. The attacking US forces also benefited from naval and air supremacy. A key factor was also the courage and offensive spirit of the troops that made up the landing forces.

On the morning of Monday, 19 February, the operation to capture Iwo Jima, code-named Operation *Detachment*, commenced. The amphibious assault was preceded by a three-day preliminary bombardment during which underwater demolition teams checked the beaches and surf conditions, searched for and destroyed obstacles in the approaches to the beaches and collected soil samples for examination onboard ship. At 09.02 the first wave of troops arrived on the assault beach carried in amphibious tracked landing vehicles, a mere two minutes after the designated 09.00 time for H-Hour.

What followed were thirty-six days of intense fighting against determined and fanatical Japanese defenders who mostly fought stubbornly to the end, preferring death to surrender. The capture and occupation phase of the Iwo Jima operation was announced complete at 08.00 on 26 March. Efforts to entirely clear the island of Japanese defenders continued, however, well into April.

The operation to take Iwo Jima would become not only one of the major actions to take place during the war in the Pacific, but an iconic part of American history. The images in this book aim to reflect this story. To describe the events relating to the capture, occupation and subsequent offensive operations that took place after the island was successfully captured would take many volumes. It is not the intention of this publication to do so. Much of the history and the many aspects of the operation have been already been covered in detail by other authors.

It is the aim of this book to tell the story using images as the main narrative. In many cases these pictures tell their own story. They are more than simple black and white photographs; they are frozen moments in time.

The combat photographers who took them left a great legacy, as did those who are captured in the images. They formed part of a remarkable generation to which all subsequent generations should be grateful. We must never forget their sacrifices.

*Mark Khan, 2018*

Note on images: All images that are uncredited are sourced from the US national archives. All other images are sourced as credited in the text related to the actual image.

# Chapter One

# The Island

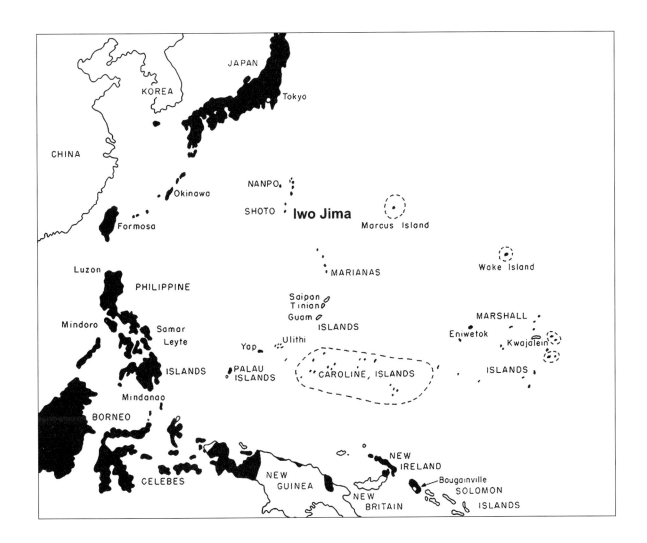

The Bonin Islands were colonized by Japan in the mid-nineteenth century. However, seafarers from Spain, Great Britain, Russia and Japan had sailed past and noted the islands from as early as the mid-sixteenth century.

The civilian population, who were all of Japanese descent, lived mostly on the central and northern part of the island. Government signs were erected around the island in 1937 warning visitors that trespassing, surveying, photographing, sketching, modeling, etc, without previous official permission was prohibited under Japanese military secrets law and that any offender would be punished. In 1943 the population on Iwo Jima numbered 1,091. Many were engaged in working at a sugar processing plant and a sulphur refinery. Others worked as fishermen and farmers. Rice, the staple diet of the Japanese, could not be grown and had to be imported. Drinking water was obtained by catching rain water in concrete cisterns. The civilian population was evacuated in June 1944 when preparations to defend the island commenced. Some of the male population remained, however, as a result of being conscripted to work on the island's defences. It was to become a fortress with no escape for most of the Japanese defenders.

Iwo Jima seen from the southern part of the island. The dormant volcano known as Mount Suribachi can be seen in the foreground. Rising to approximately 550ft, it dominates the island. The summit of the volcano is approximately the same height as the Washington Monument or the Post Office Tower in London. (USN)

The island viewed from the south-west. Taken before the invasion began, the Japanese' two airfields in the centre of the island can be seen. A patchwork of fields can also be made out around the southern tip of the island. These would be destroyed by the massive preliminary bombardment by air and sea, which started in June 1944 and ended with the intensive three-day period prior to the assault and subsequent bombardment supporting the assault on the island. (USN)

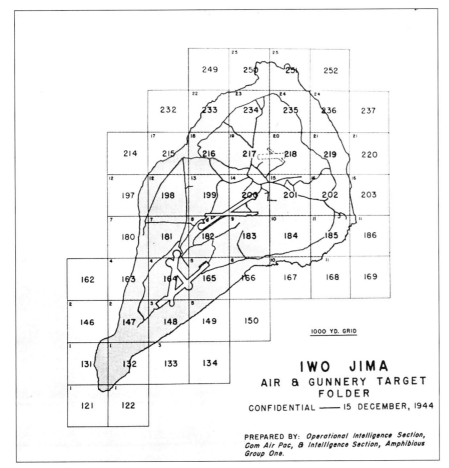

IWO JIMA
AIR & GUNNERY TARGET
FOLDER
CONFIDENTIAL —— 15 DECEMBER, 1944

PREPARED BY: *Operational Intelligence Section,
Com Air Pac, & Intelligence Section, Amphibious
Group One.*

An important part of the preliminary assault preparations was intelligence work to identify the defences on Iwo Jima. This was carried out using air photography and air photography interpretation. The island was divided into grid squares to define the location of defences and to allow these to be destroyed by bombardment from the sea and the air. This map shows the main grid square locations. Each of these squares were broken down into twenty-five smaller squares identified by an A–Y suffix.

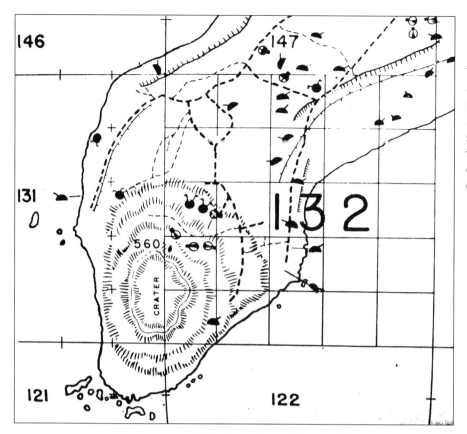

This map details part of the area around Mount Suribachi. Detailed as grid square '132', the twenty-five sub-division grid squares can be seen.

Each defined map area was accompanied by an aerial photograph. This image covers the same area to accompany the map of grid square '132'.

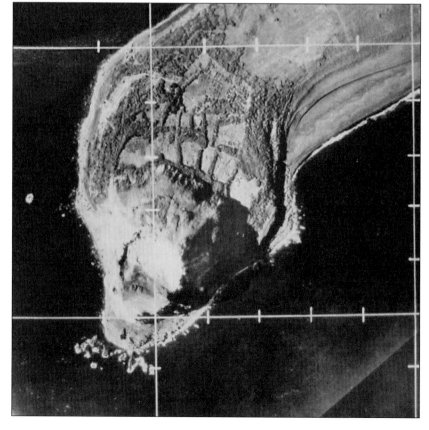

One of the many air photo reconnaissance photos taken prior to the assault on Iwo Jima details the southern end of Motoyama No.1 Airfield. Aircraft can be seen ranged on the airfield. Extensive preliminary bombardment eventually made it impractical for the Japanese to operate aircraft from Iwo Jima, and the last organized supply flight occurred on 10 February 1945. Five Mitsubishi G4M Betty bombers few in supplies and evacuated wounded men. Whilst on the ground they were attacked by six P-38 fighters of the 19th and 333rd fighter squadrons of the US 7th Air Force, which were conducting a photo reconnaissance and fighter sweep over the island. Two of the bombers were shot down and another damaged. (USN)

The architect of the defences of Iwo Jima was Lieutenant-General Tadamichi Kuribayashi. A pragmatic, experienced and professional soldier, Kuribayashi had served as deputy military attaché to Washington, D.C. in 1928.

Over a period of eight months, under his direction the island was turned into a formidable defensive fortress comprising of extensive subterranean facilities, more than 900 major gun installations and several thousand different types of defensive fighting positions.

The brilliance of Kuribayashi's defensive plan for the island is hard to overestimate. Each of Iwo Jima's cross-island defensive belts contained several 'anchor' hills or ridges that had been hollowed out with reinforced caves, barracks, undetectable pillboxes, and blockhouses with multiple entrances. Positions in and around these anchor defenses were connected by subterranean passageways. Kuribayashi had hoped to dig seventeen miles of tunnels, connecting all of his defense sectors deep underground, but our arrival interrupted his work in progress. About eleven miles had been completed when we landed. The system allowed for the defenders when attacked from one direction to quickly shift to alternative positions; they could then lay down fire on the rear and flanks of the attackers. The approaches to these anchor defenses were also covered by mutually supporting machine-gun nests and riflemen hidden in spider holes.

*Major General Fred Haynes USMC Retd.*

General Kuribayashi planned to defend the island using a strategy of attrition. The enemy was not to be engaged whilst on the beaches, but when he came across the multiple defences behind the beaches. There would also be no suicidal charges (sometimes referred to as 'General Attacks'). He regarded these as wasteful and self-defeating.

To the defenders of Iwo Jima, he issued a document titled *The Oaths of Combat.* This stated:

1) We will wield all of our strength to protect this island.
2) We will carry explosives and pulverize the enemy tanks into dust.
3) We will rush into the enemy's midst as kirikoni-tai (a type of quick, rushing attack) to annihilate them.

4) We will hit our targets, killing an enemy with each shot.
5) We will not die until we have each taken ten enemy lives.
6) We will hold out using guerrilla warfare to harass the enemy.

A realist, Kuribayashi realized that there would be no victory for the Japanese garrison. For most it would be their tomb.

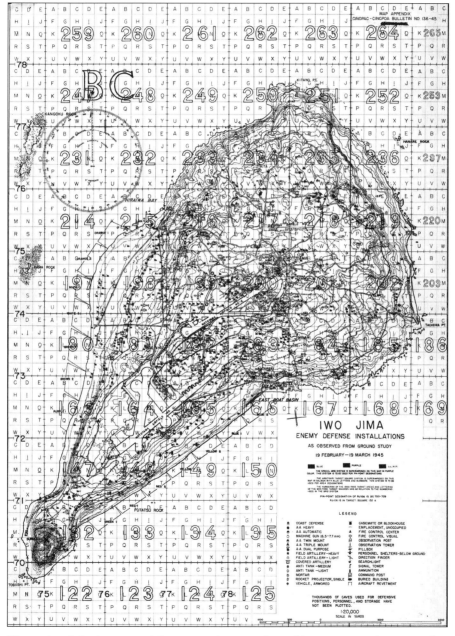

The scale of the Japanese defences can be seen from this map created as part of a ground study. Hundreds of positions have been plotted. The location of these defences utilized the terrain to provide interlocking fields of fire.

# Chapter Two

# The Photographers

Many of the images in this book were taken by United States Marine Corps combat cameramen. Marines first, cameramen second, they landed and took part in action at Iwo Jima. Approximately sixty marine combat cameramen landed with the US Marines. One of these cameramen was United States Marine Corps Staff Sergeant William Homer 'Bill' Genaust, pictured left in the image below on Iwo Jima with Corporal Atlee S. Tracey.

Bill Genaust enlisted in the Marine Corps on 11 February 1943. After training as a Marine at Quantico, Virginia, he went on to become a Marine Corps still photographer and motion picture camera photographer. Bill served with the Marines during the invasion of Saipan in July 1944 and was wounded in the leg. After an eight-month recovery period, he was given the chance of going home, but elected to stay and volunteered to take part in the amphibious assault on Iwo Jima. Bill landed on Iwo Jima with the 4th Marine Division on 19 February 1945, and captured what are now considered iconic moving picture images.

On 23 February a forty-man patrol consisting primarily of members of Third Platoon, Company E, 2nd Battalion, 28th Marines, 5th Marine Division led by 1st Lieutenant Harold Schrier climbed to the summit of Mount Suribachi and secured an American flag. This moment was captured by US Marine Corps Staff Sergeant Louis Lowery. A second larger flag was raised on Mount Suribachi later on the same day – this moment, captured as a still image by Associated Press photographer Joe Rosenthal, would become one of the iconic images of the battle for Iwo Jima. Bill Genaust was present during the second flag raising and captured the moment using colour cine film. Bill was later killed on Iwo Jima on 4 March by enemy small arms fire whilst entering a cave. His body has never been recovered. He was posthumously awarded a Bronze Star for his part in action during a firefight on Saipan on 9 July 1944. He was recommended for the Navy Cross by his photo section commander, but the nomination was turned down because Genaust was a cameraman and not an infantryman. Bill is commemorated along with 28,809 US servicemen listed as missing in action on the Honolulu Memorial in Hawaii.

The images captured by men such as Bill Genaust and his colleagues have left an incredible legacy. Some paid the ultimate price. Without them, a book such as this would not have been possible.

# Chapter Three

# **Preparation**

When the United States declared war on Japan in December 1941 the Marine Corps had an authorized strength of only 45,000 men. It comprised two operational divisions, the 1st and 2nd, and they had been in existence less than a year. Within a short time after the commencement of US involvement in the Second World War both divisions were engaged in combat on the islands of Guadalcanal and Tulagi. The 3rd Marine Division, which was formed in September 1942, took part in operations in the northern Solomon Islands. By July 1943, the active duty strength of the Marine Corps had risen dramatically to 21,938 officers and 287,621 Marines. The Corps did not create its new divisions from scratch, but based them around a core of existing units, with a backbone as much as possible comprising veteran combat Marines. New enlistees, draftees, and reservists then filled out the ranks.

The major units making up the V Amphibious Corps tasked with assaulting Iwo Jima were three divisions of the United States Marine Corps; the 3rd, 4th and 5th Marine Divisions. They would be closely supported by units of the US Army, US Navy and United States Army Air Force.

**The 3rd Marine Division**
The 3rd Marine Division officially activated 16 September 1942 at Camp Elliott, San Diego, California. Over the period January and February 1943, the division moved from Camp Elliott to Auckland, New Zealand. The division was first employed in action in the Guadalcanal campaign. It moved to Guadalcanal in August 1943, where it took part in training and rehearsals for operations to capture the central Solomon Islands. On 1 November 1943, the division landed at Empress Augusta Bay, Bougainville, and fought for approximately two months against strong Japanese resistance until 16 January 1944, when it returned to Guadalcanal.

On 21 July 1944, the 3rd Division landed on the western beaches of Guam and took part in the savage fighting to capture the island. On 10 August 1944 Guam was declared secure. The division remained on Guam, taking part in the mopping up operations.

## 4th Marine Division

The 4th Marine Division was formally activated at Camp Pendleton on 16 August 1943. The division left San Diego on 13 January 1944, sailing to the Marshall Islands. Kwajalein Atoll was recognized as the pivotal point in the defence system of the Marshalls and the task of assaulting and capturing Roi-Namur Island in the atoll was given to the 4th Marine Division. The division landed on the island on 1 February 1944 and, after hard fighting, it was secured by 12.15 on 2 February 1944.

After the action at Roi-Namur, the division moved to Hawaii, in order to absorb replacements for the division's casualties on Kwajalein Atoll, re-equip themselves, and train for their next amphibious assault.

The next action was the assault on Saipan in the Marianas, which took place on 15 June 1944. Setting up airbases here would enable US bombers to attack the Japanese mainland. The Japanese defenders put up a determined resistance, employing counter-attacks and infiltration attempts. The island was secured on 17 June.

From Saipan the division once more returned to Hawaii for rest and preparation for the next task.

## 5th Marine Division

The 5th Marine Division was activated on Armistice Day, 11 November 1943 at Camp Pendleton, California. The division remained here, preparing for action undertaking a rigorous training regime. Over the period 22 July to 5 August 1944, the units of the division sailed for Hawaii in preparation for the assault on Iwo Jima.

The divisions based on Hawaii trained hard for their respective roles in relation to the assault. The 4th Marine Division was based at Camp Maui on the island of Maui, with the 5th Division based at Camp Tarawa located on the north-central part of the island of Hawaii.

> The training facilities prepared by the 2nd Division were in the process of being expanded and improved by Marine engineers and Seabees. After we arrived at Camp Tarawa, CT 28 already well prepared for combat, received four additional months of intensive training, focusing on small-unit tactics and innovative amphibious-assault techniques tailored to our impending attack on Iwo Jima and, more particularly, our initial objective: seizing Mount Suribachi.
>
> *Captain Fred Haynes USMC, CT 28, 5th Marine Division*

With the time for training over, on 27 January the assault convoy carrying the 4th and 5th Marine Divisions with their supporting units sailed from Pearl Harbor heading for the island of Eniwetok in the Marshall Islands. The amphibious support forces left the Island of Ulithi on 10 February. On 11 February the assault convoys arrived at Saipan. Assault rehearsals were carried out by the amphibious assault forces and the crews of the landing boats on the Island of Tinian on 12 and 13 February. The amphibious support forces along with a slow convoy of the main assault force sailed for Iwo Jima on 14 February with the main assault convoy sailing on 16 February. Most of the landing force units that staged on Guam were not scheduled to arrive on D-Day. Therefore, these troops sailed after the assault divisions left Saipan.

Slowly but surely the assault convoys headed on a northerly course with the men that would assault the beaches of Iwo Jima on D-Day, 19 February.

The departure of the Third Division for Iwo Jima was like the start of a big training exercise. We were in reserve, a well-earned change from the last two operations. 'We may not even get ashore,' Dave Jones said hopefully. 'With the Fourth and Fifth on that tiny damn island, there won't even be room for us.' We rolled up our blankets, closed our footlockers, and walked out of our tents. We would be back, simple as that. But it wasn't that simple. We were on a deadly journey into hell. For the replacements it was a thrill, the big show. For the old hands it was hell. We knew enough to be scared. The novelty went out of it in Guam or Bougainville or Guadalcanal, a month, a year, or two years ago. We got through that. Our nerves were calmed down. We could eat again, sleep again, look forward again. Now that heavy black cloud was rolling in once more. This time it was Iwo Jima.

*Lieutenant Thayer Soule, Field Photographic Unit, (USMC)*

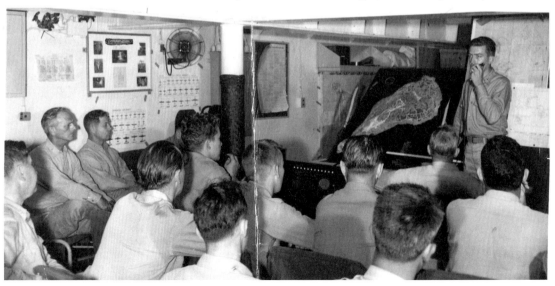

A briefing about the island. Special topographical models of Iwo Jima were constructed for this purpose. (USMC)

Shipboard days were filled with physical conditioning, letter writing, weapons cleaning, sleep, card playing, and, of course, thoughts of what lay ahead. (USMC)

Two days later Colonel Robertson called us back to the harsh realities of the impending struggle. He scheduled a meeting of all the battalion officers, to be held in the wardroom at 1330. Everyone was waiting expectantly when he entered the compartment followed by Major Mix. Donn J. Robertson was a handsome man in his late twenties, well over six feet tall, graceful and assured in movement. His unruffled exterior promoted confidence and trust, and he earned the affection of his junior officers by listening patiently to our problems. Even when exasperated, he never employed the common profanities. The colonel began with: 'Gentlemen, I have received some unsettling information today. The fourteen thousand enemy troops on the island have been recently reinforced with nine thousand new men. The other bad news is that our chief adversary will be Lieutenant General Tadamichi Kuribayashi. He is one of the foremost artillery experts in the Imperial Army. It is not likely that he will order any foolish banzai charges. They will lay back and blast us with their heavy weapons. Iwo Jima will be a tough nut to crack.'

*Lieutenant (MC) James S. Vedder, United States Navy,*
*attached 5th Marine Division*

The original caption to this image states: 'Major General C.B. Cates, commanding general of the 4th Marine Division, talks to war correspondents just prior to the assault on Iwo Jima. Left to right are: Brigadier General Franklin A. Hart; Robert Sherrod, of *Time* magazine; Keith Wheeler of the *Chicago Times*; Major General Cates; William Marien, of the *Sydney, Australia, Morning Herald*; James Lindsley, of the Associated Press; Axel Olsen, of the *Melbourne, Australia, Argus*; William Forster, of the National Broadcasting Company; Lieutenant Colonel William F. Thyson; and Colonel John L. Lanigan.' (USMC)

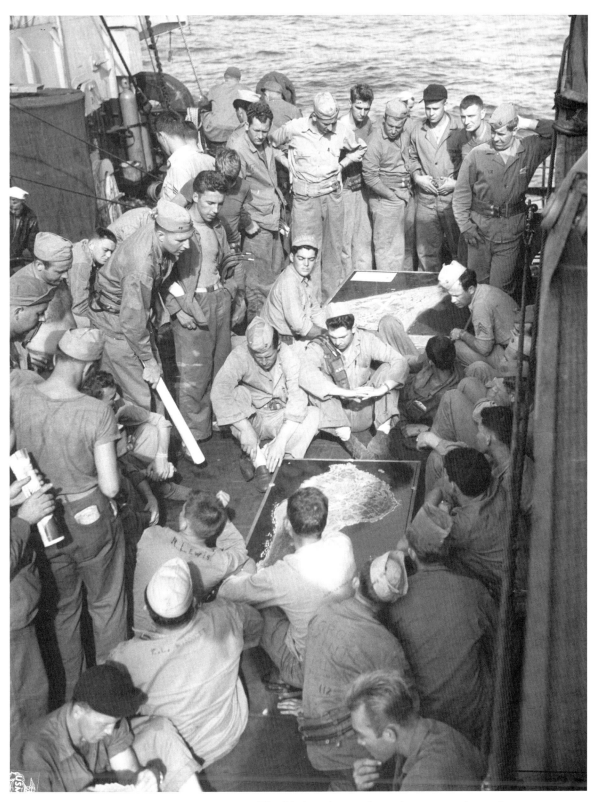

The original caption to this image states: 'The Marines knew where they were going and from briefing classes such as this one being held by Marine Captain K. Chandler, on board ship, were well acquainted with the nature of their objective, Iwo Jima.' (USMC)

Men of the 5th Marine Division, en route to Iwo Jima undergoing weapon training instruction on an M1919 .30 calibre Browning machine-gun. (USMC)

# Chapter Four

# **The Preparatory Bombardment**

It was realized well in advance of the assault landing that Iwo Jima was undoubtedly the most heavily defended island yet attacked by American forces. The appreciation of the defences grew progressively as a result of intelligence interpretation from air reconnaissance missions:

- On 1 January there were 456 located defences.
- On 3 February there were 555 located defences.
- On 8 February there were 625 located defences.
- On 13 February there were 746 located defences.

The reality was that there were even more defences than finally thought.

### The Air Bombardment

The island was first attacked on 15 June 1944 by aircraft from the carriers USS *Yorktown* and USS *Hornet*. This strike was aimed at supporting the landings taking place on Saipan by interdicting aircraft Japanese movements that might interfere with these operations.

Once the Mariana Islands had been captured, the airfield was quickly put into operation. Missions by aircraft of the 7th Air Force commenced against Iwo Jima in early July 1944 in the form of photo reconnaissance flights. The first strike mission was launched on 10 August 1944 when three squadrons of B-24 Liberators bombed the island. An increased tempo of aerial bombardment resulted in daylight bombing missions by Marianas-based bombers hitting Iwo Jima once every twenty-four hours. These strikes were accompanied by night harassing missions, fighter sweeps and further photo reconnaissance flights.

Raids by the US Army Air Force were supported by Marine bombing squadron six twelve (VMB-612), which operated from Saipan. VMB-612 flew the North American PBJ – the navalized equivalent of the Army Air Force's famous B-25 twin-engine Mitchell bomber – and operated on night sorties through the Volcano and

Bonin Islands to disrupt enemy shipping activities. Many of these night-time shipping strikes were targeted at supply traffic travelling to Iwo Jima. Using radar and equipped with air-to-ground rockets, the aircraft of VMB-612 operated with considerable success, reporting twenty-three Japanese ships sunk. Support from the air continued right up until H-hour on 19 February. After the landings had commenced, air support was subject to the air support plan set up to aid the assault.

## The Naval Bombardment

The initial plan for preliminary naval gunfire bombardment required shelling to begin from D minus 8, then to be increased from D minus 3 to H-Hour. This was based on previous experience at Tarawa, Saipan, and Peleliu, where it was deemed that preliminary bombardments had not been adequate. This bombardment period was, however, cut down to three days due to the limitations on the availability of ships, difficulty in replenishing ammunition, and the perceived loss of surprise that would result from a lengthy bombardment.

The preliminary bombardment commenced at 08.00 on 16 February. Poor weather hampered visibility, which made effective gunfire control extremely difficult. The bombardment task had been allocated to Task Force 54, comprising of the battleships USS *Tennessee*, USS *Idaho*, USS *Nevada*, USS *Texas*, USS *New York* and USS *Arkansas,* and cruisers USS *Tuscaloosa*, USS *Chester*, USS *Pensacola*, USS *Salt Lake City* and USS *Vicksburg*.

On the morning of D-Day, 19 February, the bombardment intensified. Two more battleships (USS *North Carolina* and USS *Washington* – a third, USS *West Virginia*, arrived later in the day) added 16in shells to the 14 and 12in types of the battleships already on station. Three additional cruisers (USS *Indianapolis*, USS *Santa Fe* and USS *Biloxi*) brought more 8 and 6in guns to the battle. Warships including cruisers and destroyers stood off Iwo Jima's south-eastern and south-western coasts, many of them placed to inflict a close in battering on the enemy. Rates of fire were increased, with periodic lulls to allow carrier-based airplanes to add their bombs, rockets and machine gun bullets to the attack. The *Nevada*, *Tennessee* and *West Virginia* were veterans of the attack on Pearl Harbor on 7 December 1941. The *West Virginia* had been sunk as a result of the attack and subsequently raised, repaired and returned to action. For these ships and their crews, this was an opportunity to seek retribution by bombarding the Japanese on Iwo Jima.

While the massive weight of ordnance greatly reduced Japanese defensive power, especially on and behind the landing beaches, much remained, and the enemy garrison was well sheltered in deep caves and bunkers. As two divisions of U.S. Marines began to come ashore, these soon revealed themselves in a deadly barrage of artillery, mortars and automatic weapons fire. Inland from the beaches, on Mount Suribachi to the south, and in the rugged terrain to the north, even more tough defences survived. These would have to be overcome before the island was ready to play its assigned role in the US assault on Japan's home islands.

By the morning of 17 February, the weather had cleared, and the battleships USS *Nevada*, USS *Idaho*, and USS *Tennessee* joined the bombardment.

On the morning of D-Day the emphasis shifted from the specific targets to beach preparation. This involved supporting fire from gunboats and gunfire support ships, from which mortars and rockets were fired.

## Underwater Demolition Teams

Part of the preparatory work prior to the main landing was carried out by Marine underwater demolition teams (UDTs). The role of these teams of highly trained specialists was to provide naval and troop commanders with up-to-date information on beach conditions and underwater beach defences. They achieved this by physically examining both the near shore and beach. On the morning of 17 February, supported by the battleships USS *Nevada*, USS *Idaho*, and USS *Tennessee* which moved in to 3,000 yards from shore to provide close support, the teams worked under constant fire from the Japanese defenders. The swimmers returned without incurring any casualties. The naval supporting forces were not so fortunate and suffered a number of casualties. As a result of their reconnaissance work, the UDTs were able to report that there were no underwater defences and both beach and surf conditions were suitable for a landing.

Whilst the Japanese are recognized as being highly professional in many aspects of constructing and managing the defence of Iwo Jima, one notable mistake was triggered by the work of the underwater demolition teams. Many of the Japanese gun positions had held their fire during the bombardment so as not give away their positions. Seeing the landing craft of the UDTs heading for the beach, they mistook this for the main landing and opened fire on them, disclosing their locations. This allowed the bombarding forces to shell these positions and neutralize many of them.

It was hoped that many of the plotted or subsequently accidently disclosed targets had been destroyed, or neutralized. Certainly, many had, but many remained intact and would subsequently cause severe challenges to be overcome by the landing forces.

US Army Air Force B-24 bombers of the 7th Air Force pound Iwo Jima in preparation for the assault landing. The island was heavily bombed for months prior to the invasion.

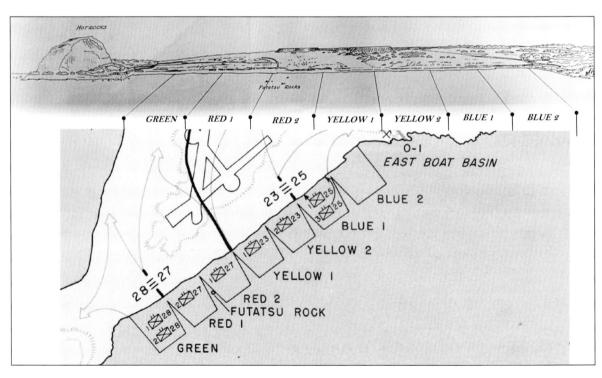

The landing beach areas. Each section was allocated to a different Marine division. The 5th Marine Division landed on Green and Red Beaches, the 4th (and later the 3rd) on Yellow and Blue beaches.

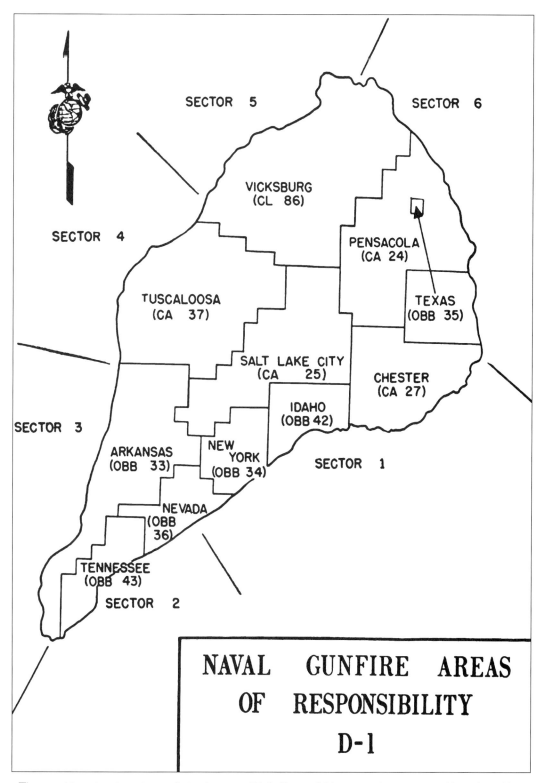

SECTOR 5

SECTOR 6

SECTOR 4

VICKSBURG
(CL 86)

PENSACOLA
(CA 24)

TEXAS
(OBB 35)

TUSCALOOSA
(CA 37)

SALT LAKE CITY
(CA 25)

CHESTER
(CA 27)

SECTOR 3

IDAHO
(OBB 42)

ARKANSAS
(OBB 33)

NEW
YORK
(OBB 34)

SECTOR 1

NEVADA
(OBB 36)

TENNESSEE
(OBB 43)

SECTOR 2

# NAVAL GUNFIRE AREAS OF RESPONSIBILITY
## D-1

The naval bombardment was allotted to naval Task Group 54 but was also supported by other ships. The allotment of different sections of the island is detailed on the (D-1) bombardment map above.

US aircraft flying over Iwo Jima. The island was pounded from both sea and air as part of the preparatory bombardment.

This image graphically illustrates the island under attack pictured from a low-flying US aircraft. (USMC)

The USS *Idaho* (BB-42) bombarding Iwo Jima. Armed with 14in guns, *Idaho* could fire high-capacity explosive projectiles weighing 1,275lb (578kg) at a rate of 1.75 rounds per minute. In this image the main armament (including the rear turret) is trained on the allotted bombardment fire area behind the Blue beaches and the East Boat Basin. (USN)

The USS *New York* (BB-34) bombarding Japanese defences on Iwo Jima, 16 February. She has just fired the left-hand 14in/45 gun of number four turret. (USN)

The 40mm guns of USS *Nevada* (BB-36) firing on the island on 17 February as part of the preparatory bombardment. Part of the ship's anti-aircraft armament, these guns could fire up to 120 rounds per minute. When firing a high explosive projectile fitted with a self-destructing fuse the range was 4,000–5,000 yards (3,700–4,570m). (USN)

Shells burst along the enemy-held shoreline of Iwo Jima during the early morning naval bombardment that preceded the landings of the Marines on the island. (USN)

About ten miles off the starboard bow was the dark hulk of Iwo Jima. We knew from our training on the way here that it was only a little porkchop-shaped island, less than five miles from south to north and two and a half miles wide at the northern end. The southern end of the island was dominated by Mount Suribachi, an extinct volcano 550 feet high. Just north of Suribachi was the narrowest part of the island, only 700 yards wide. A plain of black volcanic sand stretched northward from there for a couple of miles, giving way by the midpoint of the island to a craggy 350-foot-high plateau of volcanic rock full of ridges and gorges that had been eroded by wind and rain into fantastic shapes perpendicular to our line of advance … All we could see of the island was a continuous sparkling of naval artillery shells bursting on its surface, fired by U.S. Navy ships that lay between us and the shore. In the cold morning air the gunfire came to our ears as a steady rumble.

*Private First Class Howard N. McLaughlin Jr, 5th Marine Division*

Were the Americans trying to wake the volcano by punching a hole in it?

*Petty Officer Second Class Tsuruji Akikusa, Nanpō Shotō Kokutai,*
*South Seas Naval Air Group*

Loading 4.5in rockets aboard USS *LCI 708*, flagship of LCI Task Force 51.15.3 during D-Day. Some landing craft were specially converted to fire these rockets. Designated LCT(R), – Landing Craft Tank – rocket, these converted LCTs were designed to lay down an intensive barrage just prior to the initial assault waves landing. (USN)

The bombarding ships were engaged by Japanese guns. Shells can be seen exploding on the starboard side of small craft off Iwo Jima. Photographed from USS *Arkansas* (BB-33) on 18 February. (USN)

This image shows battle damage to USS *Pensacola* (CA-24) caused by Japanese shore batteries on Iwo Jima. *Pensacola* took six hits from enemy shore batteries as her guns covered operations of the minesweepers close inshore. On 17 February, three of her officers and fourteen men were killed. Another five officers and 114 men were injured. (USN)

Part of the preparation work was carried out by Marine underwater demolition teams. On 17 February, the reconnaissance platoon from Underwater Demolition Team 15 leaves APD *Blessman*. Attached to the side of an LCPR (landing craft, personnel, ramped) is one of the team's LCR(s) (landing craft, runner, small) in position for launching and recovery of swimmers.

White phosphorus rounds burst ashore as destroyers prepare for an underwater demolition team operation off Iwo Jima's West Beach on 17 February. Note the Fletcher-class destroyer, photographed from USS *Texas* (BB-35), firing in support very close to the shore. (USN)

For actions in supporting the underwater demolition teams, Lieutenant (Junior Grade) Rufus G. Herring, U.S. Naval Reserve, would be the first person to be awarded the Congressional Medal of Honor during the battle to capture Iwo Jima. The official after-action report by the Commander Underwater Demolition Teams stated: 'The combatant spirit of the LCI(G)s, and their cold deliberate courage was inspiring and deserved of all praise and recognition.'

Herring's citation states:
For conspicuous gallantry and intrepidity at the risk of his life above and beyond the call of duty as commanding officer of LCI (G) 449 operating as a unit of LCI (G) Group 8, during the pre-invasion attack on Iwo Jima on 17 February 1945. Boldly

closing the strongly fortified shores under the devastating fire of Japanese coastal defence guns, Lieutenant (then Lieutenant (j.g.)) Herring directed shattering barrages of 40mm. and 20mm. gunfire against hostile beaches until struck down by the enemy's savage counterfire which blasted the 449's heavy guns and whipped her decks into sheets of flame. Regaining consciousness despite profuse bleeding he was again critically wounded when a Japanese mortar crashed the conning station, instantly killing or fatally wounding most of the officers and leaving the ship wallowing without navigational control. Upon recovering the second time, Lieutenant Herring resolutely climbed down to the pilothouse and, fighting against his rapidly waning strength,

Lieutenant (Junior Grade) Rufus G. Herring.

took over the helm, established communication with the engine room, and carried on valiantly until relief could be obtained. When no longer able to stand, he propped himself against empty shell cases and rallied his men to the aid of the wounded; he maintained position in the firing line with his 20mm. guns in action in the face of sustained enemy fire and conned his crippled ship to safety. His unwavering fortitude, aggressive perseverance, and indomitable spirit against terrific odds reflect the highest credit upon Lieutenant Herring and uphold the highest traditions of the U.S. Naval Service.

# Chapter Five

# The Run-in

In the early hours of 19 February, the ships carrying the attack force and the amphibious support forces arrived off Iwo Jima. Comprising more than 450 ships, this vast armada was larger than any before assembled for an operation in the Pacific.

The weather that morning was good with clear skies providing unlimited visibility, and a gentle breeze from the north. Aboard the assault vessels, those destined to land on the beaches clambered aboard the hundreds of seaborne craft and amphibious vehicles. It was something the veterans taking part had experienced before, and had practised many times.

The launching signal was given at 07.25. The landing force, which included 482 Amtracs (amphibious assault vehicles) carrying eight battalions of Marines, headed toward the beach.

At 08.05 the guns of the naval bombardment force lifted their fire as fighter and bomber aircraft swept in to attack the island with rockets, bombs and machine guns. During this phase of the attack the gunfire support ships moved in closer to shore in readiness to support the landing.

The line of departure for the landing force was 4,000 yards from the shore. The naval bombardment now continued to fire on the beaches over the heads of the successive waves of advancing landing craft and Amtracs. At 08.57, with the leading waves nearing their objectives, the naval gunfire shifted inland and to the flanks.

The first wave of the LVT(A)s (landing vehicle tracked, armoured) hit the beach at Iwo Jima at 09.02, two minutes after the actual planned time. This was followed three minutes later at 09.05 by the second wave (the first of the troop-carrying waves). The Marines had landed.

As we stood waiting at attention, the sky brightened in the east. It was going to be a calm, clear day. A few minutes later, as the sun appeared over the horizon, we could see the silhouette of Iwo Jima clearly outlined twelve miles to the west. Mount Suribachi to the south stood out as the highest point on the island. The bare rock of Suribachi's summit, 556 feet high, reflected back

Amtracs loaded with Marines emerge from the depths of a Coast Guard-manned *LST 787* at the right and surge toward shore on D-Day. (USN)

the first rays of the sun. In just a few hours, we would be landing three hundred yards north of this eminence on Red Beach 2. At this moment the debarkation officer called out, 'All men in boat team 21 over the rail. Your boat is alongside.' I slid over the rail clutching the hemp strands of the net. I felt unbalanced and top-heavy. Except for my heavy boots, all the surplus weight was located above my belt. Besides my forty-pound backpack, I was encumbered by my steel helmet, my trenching shovel, one pistol plus extra shells, one hand grenade, one canteen of water, and a gas mask filled with three oranges and three apples. If I made one misstep and fell into the water, I would sink like a stone.

*Lieutenant (MC) James S. Vedder, United States Navy,*
*attached 5th Marine Division*

Marine-laden assault craft head to the beach at Iwo Jima during the initial landings on D-Day. Note Mount Suribachi looming in the left background. (USMC)

As we got closer to Iwo Jima, it was to our disbelief to see Mt. Suribachi being bombarded so heavily by Navy gunfire from our battleships, destroyers, cruisers and other artillery boats. A steady stream of rockets just pounded Mt. Suribachi. This was being backed up by single engine dive bombers who would dive into the depths of the dead volcano walls dropping their bombs and then with their engines roaring would scream back out skyward.

*Sergeant John Ryland Thurman USMC, 27th Regiment, 5th Marine Division*

The assault seen from the air. The first assault wave can be seen be seen approaching the beach, with the second wave following closely.

As the landing craft motored for the shore, the drone of the engines drowned out the voices of the assault Marines. Yells, hand signals, and facial expressions were the modes of communication as the crucial moment approached. Men looked at their squad mates with reassuring grins or thrust their thumbs in the air, and some men shouted phrases of encouragement – as much for their own benefit as of their fellow Marines.

*Captain Fred Haynes USMC, CT 28, 5th Marine Division*

Marines of the 4th Division landing on Iwo Jima on D-Day despite the hail of mortar and light artillery fire the stubborn enemy defenders are raining down on the beachhead. Two attack waves are advancing up the barren slope toward the first airfield, while a third assault line has just left the beach. Other waves await their turn and still more troops are headed shoreward in landing craft. (USMC)

# Chapter Six

# On the Beach

The first wave comprising of LVT(A)s armed with close-support 75mm guns mounted in turrets hit the beach at 09.02. Their task was to manoeuvre off the beach and provide fire support for the second wave, which comprised the landing troops. The terrace immediately behind the beach, in places as high as 15ft, masked enemy fire directly onto the beach but proved to be impassable to many of the LVTs. They were forced to remain on the beach giving covering fire to the landing of troops and engaging inland targets from the water.

At 0905 the second wave landed on the beaches and the Marines stormed ashore. The 5th Division landed on Green and Red One and Red Two beaches on the left side of the landing beach. The 4th Division landed abreast Yellow One, Yellow Two and Blue One beaches.

As the troops landed they moved forward and had to climb the incline formed by the terrace immediately behind the beach. The beaches themselves were not heavily manned as the Japanese defenders were dug in and waiting in emplacements inland.

As the Marines attempted to move away from the beach, they were subjected to heavy, accurate and sustained enemy fire. Congestion along the shore mounted. Pinned down on the beach, the Marines had to try to move off it. Attacking the inland defences with grit, determination and courage, that is just what they did. Pressing home their attacks, they started to advance inland. The battle for Iwo Jima now began in earnest.

Chills ran up our back when we first laid foot on the black sand, sinking up over our ankles. We did not know what to expect and it was like pulling our feet out of thick mud. We knew there would be no digging foxholes in this stuff, were to keep moving in and take ground. It looked like we had about a twenty-foot bank in front of us to climb up and more black sand. Walking took three steps to one clawing our way up. Just as I got to the top, I was hit, knocking me to the ground, I felt a sharp pain in my hip. I rolled over to take a look. I discovered a piece of shrapnel that had just gone thru my canteen leaving a hole about the size of a ping pong ball. It also went right thru my canteen cup stopping right at my hip. The canteen had a bulge in it but no penetration to its sides. I could hear the shrapnel rattle inside my canteen. I was lucky, it nearly made it thru and there was no wound. I got to my feet to get out of there and I didn't get too far when I heard someone calling out for help. I looked over to my side and I saw a fellow Marine was down on his knee trying to get his backpack off. His whole backside was smouldering with smoke, he had been hit by a phosphorous shell and his left arm was in bad shape, nearly useless. I got a hold of his backpack and used the protective material where ever I could to keep the phosphorous from burning my own hands. I was able to get most of the flesh burning phosphorus off, but he still moaned with every move. Another Marine came up to give me a hand. We continued to try and pick the stuff off with our K-bar and spread some sand on him, but that didn't help very much. We were very glad to see a Navy Corpsman show up as he asked us to hold him down while he spread some powder on the Marine. Then he told us, 'I'll take it from here, you guys get going.'

*Sergeant John Ryland Thurman USMC, 27th Regiment, 5th Marine Division*

So we got out [of our boat] and got our feet wet, and sure enough the beach was absolutely packed. I waved at my men to come on and we went up through the groups, I don't know how far but it was a fair distance, fifty feet or something like that. Then we plunked down, we were all loaded [with equipment] and the beach sand was volcanic and very hard to walk in. The artillery fire was getting pretty heavy at this point, there was machine-gun fire, and there was a whole lot of activity that was going on right where we landed. Right next to where I dropped down there was a Marine I didn't know. He was dead, and another guy right next to him had just gotten wounded, so it was obvious to me that we had to get out. About that time we were all lying together, just hordes of men—the beach was literally covered with men—and suddenly I saw Liversedge (Colonel Harry B. Liversedge, Commander 28th Marine Regiment) and Williams (Lieutenant-Colonel Robert Williams, Executive Officer 28th Marine Regiment) walk up the beach as if they were in the middle of a parade. Williams had his riding crop, which he was slapping on the side of his leg, and both of them were urging us on, saying, 'Get up! Get up! Get off the damn beach!' It was an amazing thing. They walked the length of that doggone [Green] beach yelling at the men, and the Marines just did it—they got right up and started to move. Of course, it jarred me as well, and

I got up, and we got over the high ground. Suddenly we were in the middle of this damn battle and there were casualties like nothing you'd ever seen.

*1st Lieutenant Greeley Wells, CT 28, 5th Marine Division*

There were so many of them … It reminded me of a crowd of baseball fans waiting for the stadium to open. I saw their numbers swell from several hundred to a few thousand. Each new wave piled on top of the last one … The beaches were so full of men, boats and vehicles that there was no way to miss them. Many were forced back into the water. Yet, I saw many small boats coming and going, bringing even more Marines.

*Petty Officer Second Class Tsuruji Akikusa, Nanpō Shotō Kokutai,*
*South Seas Naval Air Group*

Chaos on the beaches, with damaged and destroyed equipment littered around. In this image a Cleaver-Brooks 2½-ton amphibious trailer can be seen on the beach. These trailers were towed behind the amphibious DUKWs. (USMC)

Marines stream ashore on 19 February. The incline behind the beach can clearly been seen in the distance. Providing cover from inland, it proved an obstacle to the troops attempting to manoeuvre away from the beach. (USMC)

In the face of withering enemy fire, 5th Division Marines work their way up the slope from Red Beach One. (USMC)

In the shadow of Suribachi. As the pall of smoke from the battlefield shrouds Mount Suribachi in the background, an afternoon assault wave of Marines makes its way over the crest of the beach terrace. This image shows how dominating was Mount Suribachi. The extinct volcano was heavily defended. The Japanese emplaced on this dominating feature were able to observe the Marines landing on the beach and pour fire onto them. (USMC)

Another view of the beach. In this image Japanese defensive fire can be seen falling in the water just off the beach. (USMC)

The original caption to this image states: 'SLOW GOING – Hitting the beach on Iwo Jima, U.S. Marine troops on D-Day are forced to hug the slender protection of the ground and creep forward on their stomachs because of the intense enemy mortar and artillery barrages hitting their position.' (USMC)

These Marines are taking cover from the heavy fire coming from the Japanese defenders. In true Marine fashion, they rallied and moved off the beach to attack the inland defences. (USMC)

Marines burrow in the volcanic sand of the Iwo beach as their comrades unload supplies and equipment from landing vessels despite the hail of fire from enemy positions on Mount Suribachi in the background. *LSM* (Landing Ship Medium) *264* and *LSM 266* can be seen unloading men and equipment. *LSM 264* was carrying men of the 5th Division, including the 5th Pioneer Battalion, 5th Motor Transport Battalion, 5th Engineer Battalion, 27th Replacement Battalion and the 31st Naval US Naval construction Battalion. (USMC)

Hauling ammunition. With enemy fire screaming overhead, Marines haul an ammunition cart on the beach at Iwo Jima on D-Day. An LCVP (landing craft vehicle personnel) from the attack transport USS *Highlands* (APA-119) can be seen beached on the left of the picture. (USMC)

The Congressional Medal of Honor citation of Corporal Tony Stein, US Marine Corps Reserve, Company A, 1st Battalion, 28th Marines, 5th Marine Division:

Corporal Tony Stein, U.S. Marine Corps Reserve, Company A, 1st Battalion, 28th Marines, 5th Marine Division.

For conspicuous gallantry and intrepidity at the risk of his life above and beyond the call of duty while serving with Company A, 1st Battalion, 28th Marines, 5th Marine Division, in action against enemy Japanese forces on Iwo Jima, in the Volcano Islands, 19 February 1945. The first man of his unit to be on station after hitting the beach in the initial assault, Cpl. Stein, armed with a personally improvised aircraft-type weapon, provided rapid covering fire as the remainder of his platoon attempted to move into position. When his comrades were stalled by a concentrated machinegun and mortar barrage, he gallantly stood upright and exposed himself to the enemy's view, thereby drawing the hostile fire to his own person and enabling him to observe the location of the furiously blazing hostile guns. Determined to neutralize the strategically placed weapons, he boldly charged the enemy pillboxes 1 by 1 and succeeded in killing 20 of the enemy during the furious single-handed assault. Cool and courageous under the merciless hail of exploding shells and bullets which fell on all sides, he continued to deliver the fire of his skilfully improvised weapon at a tremendous rate of speed which rapidly exhausted his ammunition. Undaunted, he removed his helmet and shoes to expedite his movements and ran back to the beach for additional ammunition, making a total of 8 trips under intense fire and carrying or assisting a wounded man back each time. Despite the unrelenting savagery and confusion of battle, he rendered prompt assistance to his platoon whenever the unit was in position, directing the fire of a half-track against a stubborn pillbox until he had effected the ultimate destruction of the Japanese fortification. Later in the day, although his weapon was twice shot from his hands, he personally covered the withdrawal of his platoon to the company position. Stout-hearted and indomitable, Cpl. Stein, by his aggressive initiative sound judgment, and unwavering devotion to duty in the face of terrific odds, contributed materially to the fulfilment of his mission, and his outstanding valor throughout the bitter hours of conflict sustains and enhances the highest traditions of the U.S. Naval Service.

The Congressional Medal of Honor citation of Sergeant Darrell Samuel Cole, U.S. Marine Corps Reserve, Machine-gun Section of Company B, 1st Battalion, 23rd Marines, 4th Marine Division:

Sergeant Darrell Samuel Cole, U.S. Marine Corps Reserve, Machinegun Section of Company B, 1st Battalion, 23rd Marines, 4th Marine Division.

For conspicuous gallantry and intrepidity at the risk of his life above and beyond the call of duty while serving as leader of a Machinegun Section of Company B, 1st Battalion, 23rd Marines, 4th Marine Division, in action against enemy Japanese forces during the assault on Iwo Jima in the Volcano Islands, 19 February 1945. Assailed by a tremendous volume of small-arms, mortar and artillery fire as he advanced with 1 squad of his section in the initial assault wave, Sgt. Cole boldly led his men up the sloping beach toward Airfield No. 1 despite the blanketing curtain of flying shrapnel and, personally destroying with hand grenades 2 hostile emplacements which menaced the progress of his unit, continued to move forward until a merciless barrage of fire emanating from 3 Japanese pillboxes halted the advance. Instantly placing his 1 remaining machinegun in action, he delivered a shattering fusillade and succeeded in silencing the nearest and most threatening emplacement before his weapon jammed and the enemy, reopening fire with knee mortars and grenades, pinned down his unit for the second time. Shrewdly gauging the tactical situation and evolving a daring plan of counter-attack, Sgt. Cole, armed solely with a pistol and 1 grenade, coolly advanced alone to the hostile pillboxes. Hurling his 1 grenade at the enemy in sudden, swift attack, he quickly withdrew, returned to his own lines for additional grenades and again advanced, attacked, and withdrew. With enemy guns still active, he ran the gauntlet of slashing fire a third time to complete the total destruction of the Japanese strong point and the annihilation of the defending garrison in this final assault. Although instantly killed by an enemy grenade as he returned to his squad, Sgt. Cole had eliminated a formidable Japanese position, thereby enabling his company to storm the remaining fortifications, continue the advance, and seize the objective. By his dauntless initiative, unfaltering courage, and indomitable determination during a critical period of action, Sgt. Cole served as an inspiration to his comrades, and his stout hearted leadership in the face of almost certain death sustained and enhanced the highest tradition of the U.S. Naval Service. He gallantly gave his life for his country.

# Chapter Seven

# The Battle for the Island

Following the assault landing on 19 February, the men of the US V Amphibious Corps commenced the task of capturing the island and defeating its Japanese defenders. It would be a gruelling battle that would last twenty-six days before organized Japanese defence was recognized to have ended at 08.00 on Friday, 16 March.

The break-out from the landing beaches required the 5th Marine Division to attack the south-western part of the island. This included the key feature, Mount Suribachi. The volcano was secured on the early morning of Friday, 23 February. As with the whole island, however, when areas were captured, groups and stragglers of Japanese defenders continued to resist and often required clearing out of sealed underground defences.

The 4th Marine Division attacked the north-east part of the island and was joined in this task by the 3rd Marine Division, which landed on the island on Saturday, the 24th.

The fight to capture Iwo Jima was bitter. The Japanese defences were carefully constructed with interlocking fields of fire and supported by deep underground tunnel and bunker systems. The geography of the island was ideally suited to defence and required the Marines and their supporting units to fight in difficult and varying terrain. Away from the beaches, rocky ravines and areas of undergrowth provided ideal cover for the Japanese and the island had to be cleared inch by inch.

The vast majority of the Japanese chose to die or be incarcerated rather than surrender. It was a gruelling and bitter battle for both attackers and defenders.

The island was officially declared secure at 18.00 on 16 March after twenty-six days of bitter fighting. Pockets of resistance still existed, however, and many small groups and individuals of Japanese carried on fighting for a long time after this,

The garrison force comprising the U.S Army 147th Infantry Regiment assumed full responsibility for the ground defence of Iwo Jima on Wednesday, 4 April.

The battle for Iwo Jima resulted in 24,891 casualties suffered by Marine, Navy and Army units. The number of fatalities (killed in action or died of wounds) came to 6,326 men.

The number of Japanese casualties is not known but is estimated to be about 21,000 killed. Some 1,083 were taken prisoner.

The actions on Iwo Jima resulted in the award of two Presidential Citations, to the assault troops of the V Amphibious Corps and to the Support Units of the V Amphibious Corps. The wording of these citations best serves as a description of the actions of the battle to capture Iwo Jima:

Presidential Unit Citation

The President of the United States takes pleasure in presenting the PRESIDENTIAL UNIT CITATION to Assault Troops of the Fifth Amphibious Corps, Reinforced United States Fleet Marine Force for service as set forth in the following:

For extraordinary heroism in action during the seizure of enemy Japanese-held Iwo Jima, Volcano Islands, February 19 to 28, 1945. Landing against resistance which rapidly increased in fury as the Japanese pounded the beaches with artillery, rocket and mortar fire, the Assault Troops of the FIFTH Amphibious Corps inched ahead through shifting black volcanic sands, over heavily mined terrain, toward a garrison of jagged cliffs, pillboxes and blockhouses commanding all approaches. Often driven back with terrific losses in fierce hand-to-hand combat, the Assault Troops repeatedly hurled back the enemy's counterattacks to regain and hold lost positions and continued the unrelenting drive to high ground and Motoyama Airfield No. 1, captured by the end of the second day. By their individual acts of heroism and their unfailing teamwork, these gallant officers and men fought against their own battle-fatigue and shock to advance in the face of the enemy's fanatical resistance; they charged each strongpoint, one by one, blasting out the hidden Japanese troops or sealing them in; within four days they had occupied the southern part of Motoyama Airfield No. 2; simultaneously they stormed the steep slopes of Mount Suribachi to raise the United States Flag; and they seized the strongly defended hills to silence guns commanding the beaches and insure the conquest of Iwo Jima, a vital inner defense of the Japanese Empire.

Presidential Unit Citation

Support Units of the Fifth Amphibious Corps United States Fleet Marine Force for service as follows:

For outstanding heroism in support of Military Operations during the seizure of enemy Japanese-held Iwo Jima, Volcano Islands, February 19 to 28, 1945. Landing against resistance which rapidly increased in fury as the Japanese pounded the beaches with artillery, rocket and mortar fire, the Support Units of the FIFTH Amphibious Corps surmounted the obstacles of chaotic disorganization, loss of equipment, supplies and key personnel to develop and maintain a continuous link between thousands of assault troops and supply ships. Resourceful and daring whether fighting in the front line of combat, or serving in rear areas or on the wreck-obstructed beaches, they were responsible for the administration of operations and personnel; they rendered effective fire support where Japanese pressure was greatest; they constructed roads and facilities and maintained communications under the most difficult and discouraging conditions of weather and rugged terrain; they salvaged vital supplies from craft lying crippled in the surf or broached on the beaches; and they ministered to the wounded under fire and provided prompt evacuation to hospital ships. By their individual initiative and heroism and their ingenious teamwork, they provided the unfailing support vital to the conquest of Iwo Jima, a powerful defense of the Japanese Empire.

A direct hit on a Marine Amtrac close to the beach. The sandbagged position appears to be part of an artillery position. An MIAI 75mm Pack Howitzer can be seen emplaced to the right of the main sandbagged position. (USMC)

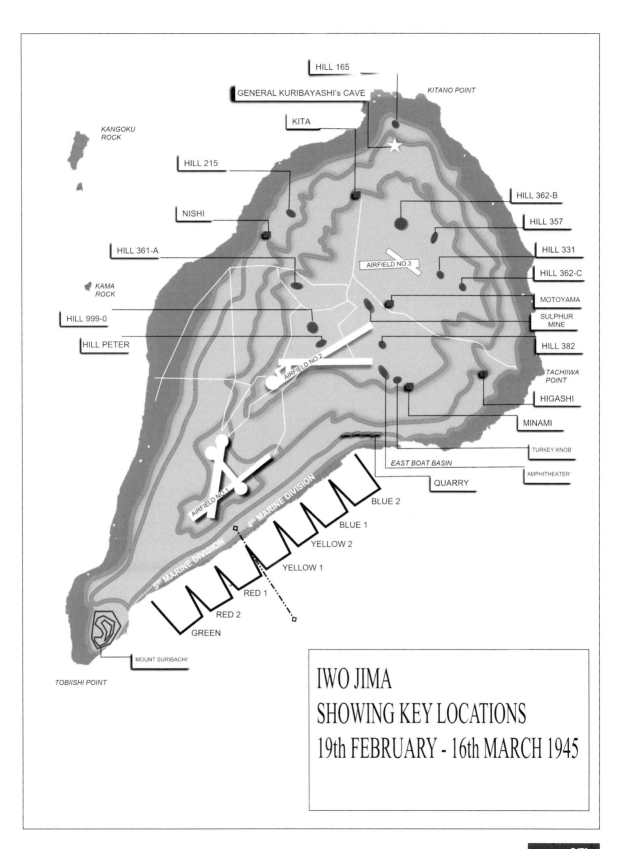

IWO JIMA
SHOWING KEY LOCATIONS
19th FEBRUARY - 16th MARCH 1945

47

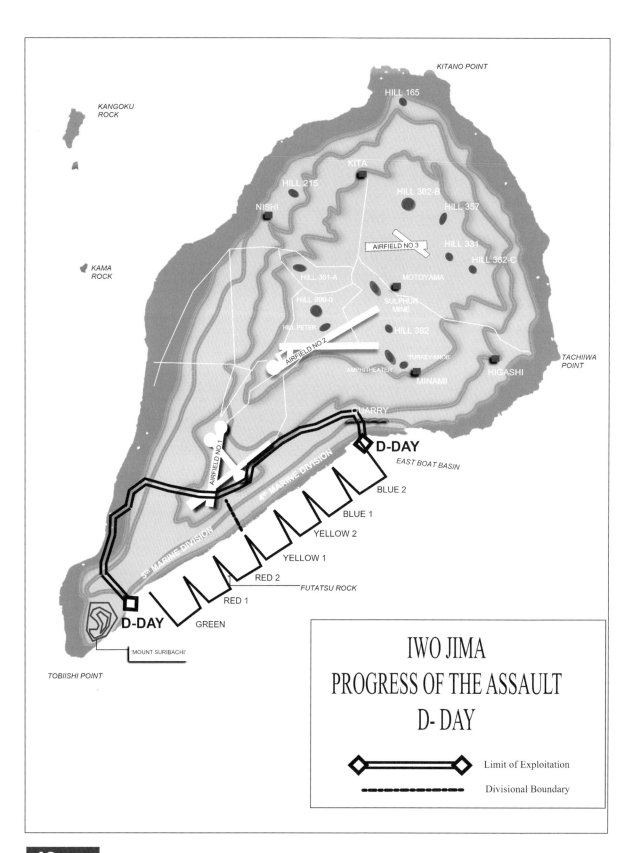

KITANO POINT

HILL 165

KANGOKU ROCK

KITA

HILL 215

HILL 362-B

HILL 357

NISHI

AIRFIELD NO.3

HILL 331

HILL 362-C

KAMA ROCK

HILL 361-A

MOTOYAMA

HILL 999-0

SULPHUR MINE

HILL PETER

AIRFIELD NO.2

HILL 382

TURKEY KNOB

'AMPHITHEATER'

MINAMI

HIGASHI

TACHIIWA POINT

QUARRY

D-DAY

EAST BOAT BASIN

AIRFIELD NO.1

4ᵗʰ MARINE DIVISION

BLUE 2

BLUE 1

YELLOW 2

YELLOW 1

5ᵗʰ MARINE DIVISION

RED 2

RED 1

FUTATSU ROCK

GREEN

D-DAY

'MOUNT SURIBACHI'

TOBIISHI POINT

# IWO JIMA
# PROGRESS OF THE ASSAULT
# D-DAY

◇━━━━━◇ Limit of Exploitation

▬▬▬▬▬ Divisional Boundary

Private First Class Don Traub, 2nd Battalion, 13th Marine Regiment, was lying in a hole next to three amphibious tractors full of ammunition and described what happened when enemy fire hit one of the Amtracs:

One of them took a direct hit from an enemy gun near Suribachi, and it blew up in a tremendous explosion, sucking me out of my hole and dropping me on my head and neck. After the barrage ended, I recovered somewhat, crawled around in the open, and saw that that the entire contour of the land around me had been rearranged and pocked with shell holes strewn with mangled bodies, body parts, and countless wounded.

A Marine shelters from a violent explosion. In the distance the dominating heights of Mount Suribachi can be seen. A bulldozer can be seen on the left of the image. (USMC)

Launching the assault. A wave of Marines is organized after reaching the Iwo beachhead and preparations are made for the push inland. An LVT(A)-4 is providing support to the Marines on the beach. The LVT(A)-4 was fitted with the turret from a Gun Motor Carriage M8 and armed with a powerful 75mm M2/M3 gun, allowing it to provide fire support. Some 1,890 examples of the LVT(A)-4 were produced through 1944. (USMC)

About one thing I am convinced: for most of the Marines on Iwo Jima that first day, the need to get on with the attack, to do their part of the work, was a more powerful force than the fear of death. Intensive training and excellent leadership by squad, platoon, and company commanders were very much responsible for this fact. It's also true that Marine Corps training, in general, has a way of making you more afraid of failing to do your job than dying. I'm not the first Marine to have said this. It's widely recognized, and one of the mysterious products of Marine Corps indoctrination. So by mid-afternoon, men all along the beach were adapting, finding ways to put together fire teams, taking care of the wounded and dead, who were everywhere in plain sight. In general, we were sorting ourselves out and getting on with the business at hand. Somehow, amid the mayhem, little pockets of order and purpose emerged.

*Captain Fred Haynes USMC, CT 28, 5th Marine Division*

A Japanese pillbox on Iwo goes up in smoke when the Marine half-tracks in the foreground score a direct hit. Japanese artillery in this area (note the gun at extreme left), was previously zeroed on the landing beach and took a heavy toll of the invading Leathernecks. One of the large-calibre Japanese guns that were defending the island can be seen on the left of the picture. (USMC)

A classic image of Marines in action. Original caption: 'At a forward observation post, Marine spotters have located the exact fix on an enemy position as one of the group calls instructions to be relayed to artillery and mortar units requesting a concentration of fire on the Japanese strong point.' (USMC)

Two Marine signallers laying communications cable. This was a vitally important task to provide communications between units. An extremely dangerous job, this required laying cable under fire as well as fixing broken lines. One tool the Marine forces had in relation to communications was Navajo Indian code talkers. By communicating in their native language, information could be sent directly by voice without the need to use code, therefore facilitating much rapider communication. No Japanese could speak Navajo! (USMC)

Navajo Indians continued to be of great value in the operation. All divisions have commented most favourably upon the success of their employment as code talkers in previous operations. In this operation, Navajos were utilised in Corps Headquarters for the first time for employment as code talkers between Corps and Division Headquarters, as well as between echelons within Corps.

*The V Amphibious Corps after-action report*

The original caption details this as: 'Blue Beach 1/4th Division watch their tasks (just below the horizon) looking north to Blue 2.' The black sand of Iwo Jima is well illustrated. (USMC)

On Blue beach, Marines push inland. A massive crater caused by the preparatory bombardment is on the left. (USMC)

This image captures the chaos of the battle. An LVT-4 can be seen on fire with a Marine sheltering behind a sandbagged position. (USMC)

The original caption to this image states: 'Burdened with heavy packs and equipment Marine communicators dash for cover during the inland drive from the Iwo beachhead.' Easily noticeable by the radios and communications equipment, signallers were prime targets for the Japanese riflemen and sharpshooters. (USMC)

Marines supported by tanks advance on Mount Suribachi. This image clearly shows how this feature dominated the Island. The V Amphibious Corps after-action report stated in relation to the use of tanks on the assault: 'Tanks proved indispensable in this operation, particularly the flame-thrower and bulldozer tanks, which were required for the assault of close-in fortified positions.' (USMC)

And increasingly as the days went by, Suribachi seemed to take on a life of its own, to be watching these men, looming over them, pressing down upon them. When they moved, they moved in its shadow, under its eye. To be sure, there were hundreds of [Japanese] eyes looking at them from the mountain, but these were the eyes of a known enemy, an enemy whose intent was perfectly clear. In the end, it is probable that the mountain represented to these Marines a thing more evil than the Japanese.

*Howard M. Conner, 5th Marine Division Historian*

This photograph is attributed to Staff Sergeant M.A. Cornelius and detailed as having been taken on 21 February. Marine artillery can be seen shelling Mount Suribachi while unloading takes place on the beach. (USN)

The original caption to this image states: 'A reserve wave of the Fourth Marine Division, burrowed into the black volcanic sand of Iwo Jima, waits its turn to move up on D-Day. Almost lost in the smoke haze on the battlefield, the previous wave is charging ahead.' (USMC)

The original caption to this image states: 'DEADLY HUNT – Warily, U. S. Marines close in on an enemy dugout on Iwo Jima, in a deadly hunt for any live Jap snipers. Marines of three Marine divisions, striking at this Volcano Island, found the enemy resistance determined and fanatical.' (USMC)

The problem for the infantry and demolitions squads in crossing the isthmus and cutting off Suribachi was that the enemy positions were mind-bogglingly numerous and mutually supporting. The fire teams laying down suppressive fire for the Marines conducting the assault had to make sure that the covering fire not only blanketed the main pillbox under attack, but also those that were supporting it. All too often we didn't know where these were initially, and that's when we could take five or six casualties in a matter of a few seconds. We were most successful when we could provide an envelope of fire around the attacking infantry to keep the mutually supporting defensive positions quiet as we moved west.

*Captain Fred Haynes USMC, CT 28, 5th Marine Division*

A Marine mortar team engage the enemy with an 81mm mortar. High-explosive and white phosphorus ammunition, ready for use, is stacked at the side of the emplacement. (USMC)

The original caption to this image states: 'Iwo Jima, February 24, 1945. Shelling Iwo-Section chief, Marine Private First Class R.F. Callahan calls for fire and another 155mm shell is hurled into a Japanese position.' The image shows this artillery piece at nearly full recoil. The gun crew has the next round ready to load. (USMC)

A battery of Marine M2A1 105mm howitzers in position on Iwo Jima. These guns firing at what were very short ranges for artillery provided vital support for the troops assaulting the Japanese positions. (USMC)

The original caption to this image states: 'Iwo Jima February 19, 1945. A Marine machine gunner fires at Japanese positions in support of a Leatherneck advance on Iwo Jima.' Machine-guns such as these firing in the sustained fire role were able to pour high volumes of fire onto Japanese positions. (USMC)

Marine Corporal Wes Plummer was awarded the Navy Cross for action as a machine-gunner. His citation reads:

Corporal Plummer, a machine gun squad leader, set up his weapon, single-handedly, while subjected to deadly fire from concealed enemy riflemen. The company advance had been halted by fire from enemy emplacements. Disregarding his personal safety, Corporal Plummer placed his gun on elevated, open terrain upon which a short time earlier, one machine gun had been demolished, killing one man and wounding two. For almost two hours he delivered supporting fire for the advancing troops. Though he was a constant target for … enemy rifle fire, Corporal Plummer … unaided, kept his gun in action. He managed to neutralize the enemy fire and thus assured his company of only light resistance in the advance. His courageous conduct was in keeping with the highest traditions of the United States Naval Service.

The original caption to this image states: 'A Marine rocket truck empties its launching rack of projectiles as it lays a barrage on Japanese positions on Iwo Jima. Being mobile, the rocket units used hit and run tactics during the operation, so that the enemy could never get an exact fit on their locations.' These mobile rocket launching vehicles were able to deliver a deadly barrage of 4.5in high-explosive rockets. (USMC)

Another volley of 4.5in rockets being fired. These highly mobile batteries were part of the vast array of equipment available to the US Marines on Iwo Jima. While the Japanese held the defensive advantage, it was technological advantages such as these rocket batteries that helped defeat the entrenched defenders. (USMC)

We had another dandy weapon that really did a number on the enemy and earned enough of their respect for them to respond fiercely to its use. This weapon was the rocket trucks, ¾ ton rugged trucks fitted with rocket racks on their beds. The racks were 6 x 6 arrays of 4.5-inch rockets that could be aimed together and fired in a salvo, all of them very quickly—almost instantaneously. I am not sure of how many of these trucks the Division had (maybe sixty-four or more), but they sure did a job. They would kind of 'carpet bomb' an area about the size of a football field, cleaning out just about anything above ground, and maybe some of the stuff below. Here's how it worked. After the leaders had determined the target—often requested by the companies on the line—the truck would roll up to a point of vantage and aim the rack. I am told they used the windshield wipers to fix the direction and hoisted the front of the rack to get the right elevation for distance. Then they hit the switch that set them off. At once the rockets would whoosh out with smoke and roar to their target, and the driver would get that truck out of there as fast as he could. Almost before the truck's dust had settled, the enemy mortars would blast the place where that truck had been. You never saw anything happen so fast. The moment the Nips saw that truck pull into place, or at least no later than the moment the first rocket hit its target, those mortar crews had to be cranking their guns into swift retaliation. They hated those trucks. We loved 'em.

*Private First Class Howard N. McLaughlin Jr, USMCR, 5th Marine Division*

*Above right:*
The original caption to this image states, 'This General Sherman tank on Iwo Jima was wrecked by a land mine and hit five times by Japanese artillery fire, but its Fourth Marine Division crew escaped without casualty. In turret, Sergeant James W. Reeses. Under the gun, left to right: Corporal Lynn S. Evans and Private First Class Lloyd F. Spickate. Charles H. Saulman is examining the damaged tread.' Tanks played a key role in the battle to take the island. Armed with a 75mm gun, the Sherman was able to knock out fortified Japanese positions. Tanks were also armed with flame-throwers and proved to be a particularly potent bunker-clearing weapon. The tanks were still vulnerable to Japanese anti-tank guns and to attacks by soldiers who placed explosive charges directly onto the tanks themselves, usually at the cost of their own lives. As such the tanks needed the mutual support of the Marine infantry. This example shows how additional protection has been added to the front and sides. Spare track links have been added to the front and turret, and wooded planking added to the sides to prevent magnetic explosive charges being placed on the side armour. (USN)

The original caption to this image states: 'Iwo Jima, February 25, 1945. Blast on Suribachi: A demolition charge seals the entrance to one of the many caves on the slopes of Mount Suribachi from which the Japanese poured a withering fire on the Marine beachhead.' Taken from the slopes of Mount Suribachi, this photograph shows the commanding view of the beaches the Japanese defenders had from the dormant volcano. (USMC)

On D+4, the 5th Marine Division had made good progress in advancing on Mount Suribachi. Lieutenant Colonel Chandler W. Johnson, commanding officer of the 2nd Battalion of the 28th Marines, gave the order to secure and occupy the crest. Two three-man patrols from Companies D and F were sent out to reconnoitre and probe for enemy resistance. None was encountered and the Marines reached the lip of the crater at 9.40. A forty-strong detachment from Company E was then sent to back them up, which reached the rim by 10.15. The Marines at this point encountered a group of Japanese defenders, who put up a stiff resistance. The Marines, however, found a length of pipe from the the wrecked Japanese radar station on the summit and a 54in × 28in flag was tied to the top and raised over Mount Suribachi at 10.20. Sergeant Louis R. Lowery was with Company E to record the event. (USMC)

The crater at the summit of Mount Suribachi. (USMC)

Just moments after the flag was raised we heard a roar from down below. Marines on the ground, still engaged in combat, raised a spontaneous yell when they saw the flag. Screaming and cheering was so loud and prolonged that we could hear it quite clearly on top of Suribachi. The boats on the beach and the ships at sea joined in blowing horns and whistles. The celebration went on for many minutes. It was a highly emotional, strongly patriotic moment for us all.

*Private First Class Ray Jacobs, F Company, 2nd Battalion, 28th Marines*

Soon after the first flag was raised, Colonel Johnson heard that secretary of the Navy James Forrestal [who, together with Lieutenant Gen. H. M. Smith, had just landed on the beach] had expressed a desire to have the small flag. Colonel Johnson sent 2nd Lieutenant Albert Tuttle to the beach area to find

Soon after the first flag was raised, a second flag replaced the original one. This flag came from *LST 779*, beached near the foot of Suribachi. This image captured by Sergeant Louis R. Lowery shows the two flags together. Today both of the flags raised on Mount Suribachi are preserved in the Marine Corps Museum at Quantico, Virginia. (USMC)

another flag. He planned to use it to replace the original flag, thus saving the first flag as a battalion memento. Lieutenant Tuttle had stated that the colonel, almost as an afterthought, said, 'See if you can get a larger flag.' Tuttle obtained a large ceremonial flag from LST-779.

At about that time I received an order to provide a detail to string telephone wire to the Suribachi patrol and sent Sgt. Michael Strank, Cpl. Harlon Block, PFC. Ira Hayes, and PFC. Franklin Sousley to the battalion CP. A runner from E Company, PFC. Rene Gagnon, was at the CP obtaining radio batteries for Schrier's patrol, and he joined Sergeant Strank's detail for the ascent. As they were about to depart, Colonel Johnson handed Gagnon the ceremonial flag [that Tuttle had procured], and told Strank to have Lieutenant Schrier replace the small flag and save it for the colonel Rosenthal and two

Marine photographers, Sgt. Bill Genaust and PFC. Bob Campbell. About halfway up the volcano, the photographers met Lou Lowery coming down to look for another camera. Lowery told the group that he had already photographed the flag being raised, but there was a terrific view to be seen if they continued to the top. As the photographers reached the summit they saw a group of Marines attaching a large flag to a pipe and were told that the small flag was to be replaced and kept as a souvenir. Rosenthal and Genaust backed away from the flagpole site and prepared to film the large flag being raised. Campbell moved into another position where he could capture the movement of both flags. Genaust started filming with his movie camera using color film as the Marines prepared to raise the second flag. Rosenthal was caught by surprise when the large flag started up and was lucky to snap one exposure, which was to become the famous photograph.

*Captain Dave Severance, Company Commander, E Company,*
*2nd Battalion, 28th Marines*

The raising of the second flag resulted in the iconic photograph associated with the battle to take the island of Iwo Jima. The image captured by Joe Rosenthal, an Associated Press photographer, resulted in a dramatic, beautifully composed picture symbolising an event that stirred the world and inspired a nation. The six flag raisers are recognized as: Corporal Harlon Block, Private First Class Rene Gagnon, Private First Class Ira Hayes, Private First Class Harold Schultz, Private First Class Franklin Sousley and Sergeant Michael Strank. Sadly, three of the flag-raisers were killed in action before the island was secured. Strank and Harlon were killed on 1 March. Sousley was killed on 21 March. (USMC)

In mid-morning, word spread that there were Marines up on the sides of Mount Suribachi. They were plainly visible to us down below—not many of them, so we decided that they must be just a patrol. Everybody was passing field glasses back and forth, watching as the patrol neared the top of the mountain. We lost sight of some of them for a few minutes, then a yell went up that was heard all over the island. The patrol was putting up an American flag. It was small, but we could all see it, even without field glasses. (It was shortly replaced by a bigger flag, as shown in the famous photograph by Joe Rosenthal.) There was cheering all around us—even the most cynical Marine who witnessed our flag being raised on Suribachi was touched deeply by the sight.

*Private First Class Howard N. McLaughlin Jr, USMCR, 5th Marine Division*

The original caption to this image states: 'FORMED – Organized and formed for the assault, Marines of one of the Regiments of the Fourth Marine Division under Major General Clifton B. Cates, USMC, are ready to attack the enemy held Motoyama Airfield Number One, on Iwo Jima, 500 yards inland from the beach.' (USMC)

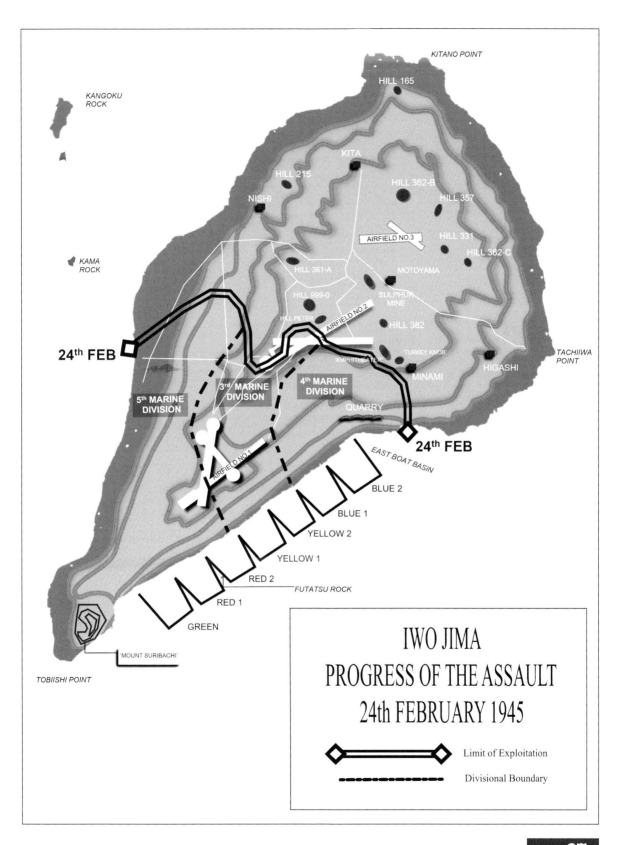

KITANO POINT

KANGOKU ROCK

HILL 165

KITA

HILL 215

HILL 362-B

HILL 357

NISHI

AIRFIELD NO.3

HILL 331

HILL 362-C

KAMA ROCK

HILL 361-A

MOTOYAMA

HILL 999-0

SULPHUR MINE

HILL PETER

AIRFIELD NO.2

HILL 382

TACHIIWA POINT

AMPHITHEATER

'TURKEY KNOB'

24th FEB

MINAMI

HIGASHI

5th MARINE DIVISION

3rd MARINE DIVISION

4th MARINE DIVISION

QUARRY

24th FEB

EAST BOAT BASIN

AIRFIELD NO.1

BLUE 2

BLUE 1

YELLOW 2

YELLOW 1

RED 2

FUTATSU ROCK

RED 1

GREEN

'MOUNT SURIBACHI'

TOBIISHI POINT

# IWO JIMA
# PROGRESS OF THE ASSAULT
# 24th FEBRUARY 1945

◇━━━━━◇ Limit of Exploitation

■━■━■━■━■ Divisional Boundary

The original caption to this image states: 'Iwo Jima February 1945. Riflemen lead the way as flame throwing Marines of the Fifth Division, crouched with the weight of their weapons, move up to work on a concentration of Japanese pillboxes.' The Japanese defenders fought a fanatical defensive campaign. One of the weapons they feared most, however, was the flame-thrower. It fired liquid fuel comprising of thickened gasoline or other various liquid oils and blends (diesel oil, light lubricating oil, cleaned crankcase drainings). Two fuel tanks contained approximately 4 gallons of flammable liquid. A third tank contained pressurised nitrogen or oxygen that was used to project the flammable liquid. In the original M1 and M1A1 models, an electrically ignited spark plug ignited the fuel as it was projected at the target. The maximum effective range was 80 yards. A flame could be maintained for ten seconds. (USMC)

The portable version with all fuel tanks filled weighed 68lb. A new cartridge-based ignition system replaced the battery version on the older model. Designated the M2-2 a five-shot, revolver-type magazine was fitted to the end of the flame tube. An ignition cartridge was utilized (for a total of five possible ignitions before reloading). The new system proved much more reliable under combat conditions. The Marine above is carrying an M2-2 version without the two fuel cylinders fitted. (USMC)

The original caption to this image states: 'DEVIL'S BREATH ON HELL'S ISLAND – Two Marine privates hit the deck to throw a scorching inferno at the mighty defenses which blocked the way to Iwo Jima's Mount Suribachi. They are, (left to right): Private Richard Klatt, of North Fondulac, Wis., and Private First Class Wilfred Voegeli.' Private Klatt is recorded as having been wounded in action in the US Marine Corps Casualty Indexes on 1 March. (USMC)

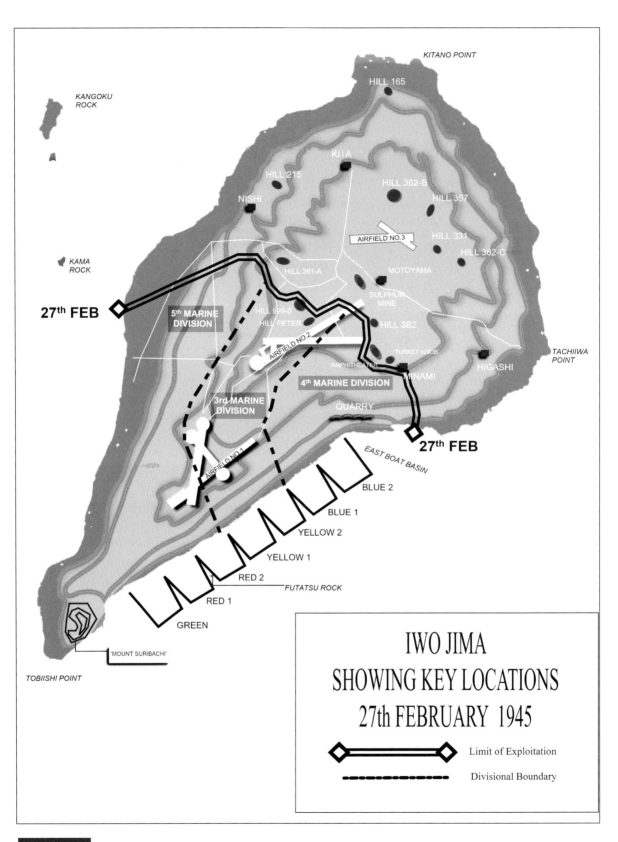

KITANO POINT

HILL 165

KANGOKU ROCK

KIIA

HILL 215

HILL 362-B

HILL 357

NISHI

AIRFIELD NO.3

HILL 331

HILL 362-C

KAMA ROCK

HILL 361-A

MOTOYAMA

SULPHUR MINE

27th FEB

5th MARINE DIVISION

HILL 999-0

HILL PETER

HILL 382

AIRFIELD NO 2

'TURKEY KNOB'

TACHIIWA POINT

'AMPHITHEATER'

4th MARINE DIVISION

MINAMI

HIGASHI

3rd MARINE DIVISION

QUARRY

AIRFIELD NO.1

EAST BOAT BASIN

27th FEB

BLUE 2

BLUE 1

YELLOW 2

YELLOW 1

RED 2

FUTATSU ROCK

RED 1

GREEN

'MOUNT SURIBACHI'

TOBIISHI POINT

# IWO JIMA
## SHOWING KEY LOCATIONS
### 27th FEBRUARY 1945

◇━━━━━◇  Limit of Exploitation

■■■■■■■  Divisional Boundary

A flame-thrower being used at close range. The operator is being covered by two of his rifleman comrades. (USN)

The original caption to this image states: 'FAITHFUL AND WAITING – while a gigantic artillery and tank battle rages behind them on the Iwo Jima beachhead, Marines (left to right) Joseph de Blanc, of Union, Maine, and PFC Frank Hall, of Reed W. Virginia, faithfully wait for orders in a shell hole.' Private First Class Frank Hall is armed with a Browning M1918A2 automatic rifle. The number of tanks that landed as part of the assaulting force totalled 138. All of these were Sherman M4A3 tanks. Of these, eight were fitted with a flame-throwing gun. (USMC)

The original caption to this image states: 'FLAME THROWER – Marine PFC John C. Georgilas, of Cambridge, Mass., (in foreground) carrying a flame-thrower, moves up with his buddies on the desolate battlefield of Iwo Jima.' PFC Georgilas is listed on the US Marine Corps Casualty Index as being wounded in action on 19 February. This image clearly shows the Marines moving into the island's interior and the changing landscape away from the beaches. As such it may have been that John Georgilas simply 'soldiered on' after being wounded. (USMC)

Carrying his M1 rifle, this Marine is said to be advancing under fire. Behind him can be seen a dead Japanese defender. (USMC)

We were now encountering increasing numbers of dead Japanese and swarms of great green flies. We figured the Japs were no longer able to reclaim their dead … The men of the 312th Independent Infantry Battalion [who defended the approaches to Suribachi] looked like first-class troops. From the scattered memorabilia that festooned the battlefield dead, we concluded that these were veterans with service in China and Southeast Asia. Japanese dead were a problem for us. Booby-trapping was endemic and some of the dead were feigning. It became necessary to shoot their dead to be sure they were. I found this coup de grace repulsive.

*Private First Class Robert Leader, E Company, 2nd Battalion, 28th Marines*

The original caption to this image states: 'DRIVE TO THE SEA – Supported by tanks, Marines stage a frontal attack on Japanese positions in the craggy ridges of northern Iwo. The blasts in the center are Jap mortar shells meant for the tank at the left. This advance netted twenty yards of ground.' As the advance inland proceeded, the support of tanks became ever more important. Able to blast out Japanese positions, the tanks still needed the mutual support of the Marine infantrymen to prevent the Japanese defenders attacking them with explosive charges. (USMC)

The Japs usually tried to disable tanks by blowing off a track with an explosive charge. Delivering the charge was a suicide mission carried out by a runner we would always call 'Satchel Charlie' because he carried the explosives in a bag not unlike the demolition pouches I had carried off the landing craft on the first day. A Satchel Charlie would pop up and dash toward the tanks at top speed, activating the delay fuse on the charge as he ran. His mission was to throw the satchel under a tank before he was killed, immobilizing it and making it easy pickings for destruction by artillery fire. Our job was to shoot anybody who approached the tanks.

*Private First Class Howard N. McLaughlin Jr, USMCR, 5th Marine Division*

A group of Marine Sherman tanks and infantrymen grouped together. The tank on the second right is a recovery version. A towing jib can be seen mounted on the rear of the hull. (USMC)

The original caption to this image states: 'THAR SHE BLOWS – Hugging the ground to escape flying debris, a Marine demolitions man sets off a charge of high explosives that blasts a Japanese pillbox on Iwo Jima. After capture, many of these positions had to be destroyed lest the enemy return to the shelters and open fire on the Marines' flanks.' This image clearly shows the close range at which these actions were required to be performed. (USMC)

We did not get too far when I heard machine gun bullets buzzing by … I kept an eye out hoping to locate the sniper as we were running … It was then that I saw my buddy to my right take a hit and going down in a heap with his ammunition box bouncing out in front of him. The machine gun bullets that hit him jerked his body to the right. So, this means the sniper had to be to our left. I looked over that way quickly taking in everything in one glance, and there I caught sight of gun smoke pouring out from under what looked like a small island of sand and rocks about for feet high … So, I circled to my right with the idea of staying out of his line of fire and at the same time work my way up behind the sniper … My plan was to tie two sticks of dynamite together with two sticks of dynamite and blow the sniper out of his nest ... I needed a way to start the fuse on fire. I was getting ready to ask for a cigarette lighter when one of the two Marines stepped up and handed me his cigarette lighter ... We dropped back at a safe distance and hit the deck. In an instant, the dynamite exploded, blowing the sniper nest wide open and forcing the insides out the front of the nest ... We didn't know what to expect. I was taken by surprise when I saw three Japanese scattered around with their air-cooled bamboo machines guns still hanging half way out of the sniper nest ... Two of the Japanese had been dead for quite some time from the looks and the smell of them, but the other sniper was still alive just before the dynamite exploded ripping the nest wide apart and him with it. His body was ripped and torn in half. His head and chest were lying with his hip and legs about ten feet away ... What really caught our attention was how this sniper stayed in the nest with two other dead snipers for what had to be quite a long time. I am sure that the smell of those two snipers had to be suffocating for him. This had to take some kind of guts ... One of the Marines was looking over at the sniper's hip and legs and noticed his wallet was hanging out of his pocket with some of his credentials lying in the sand. Just out of respect he decided to walk over there and take care of the wallet and credentials by putting them back in his pocket. In putting things together, he noticed a photograph of the sniper and his family and showed it to us. It must have been his dad, mother, brother, and sister. The sniper had his military uniform on and was looking very sharp. Everything was put back in his pocket.

*Sergeant John Ryland Thurman, 27th Regiment, 5th Marine Division*

The original caption to this image states: 'Battle for Iwo Jima, February–March 1945. Men on line tense. Photographed by Corporal Joe Schwartz, February 20, 1945.' This heavily laden young Marine is armed with a Browning automatic rifle. (USN)

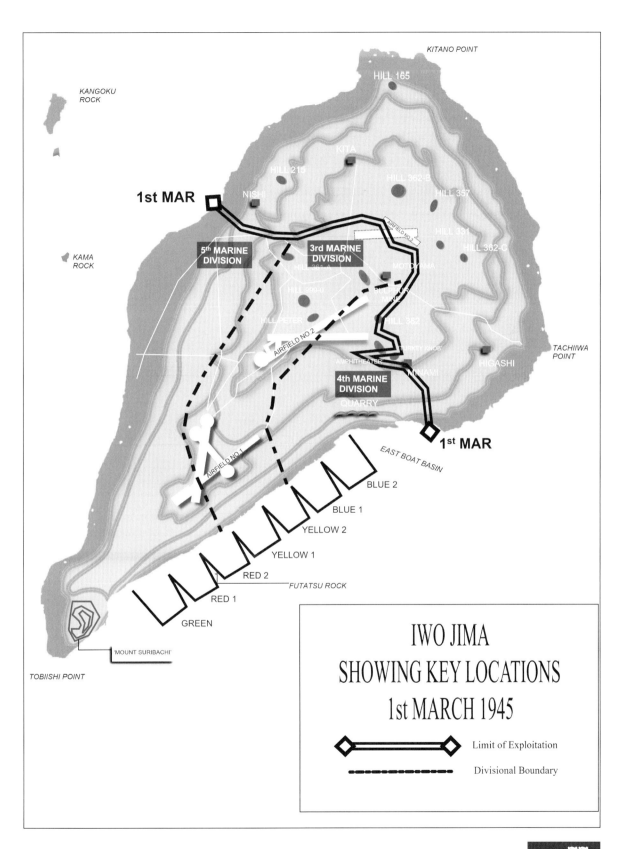

KITANO POINT

HILL 165

KANGOKU
ROCK

KITA

HILL 215        HILL 362-B
                                HILL 357

NISHI

**1st MAR**

**5th MARINE
DIVISION**          **3rd MARINE
DIVISION**

KAMA
ROCK                        HILL 361-A        AIRFIELD NO 3

HILL 331

HILL 362-C

MOTOYAMA

HILL 999-U          SUICIDE
                    MINAMI

HILL PETER                  HILL 382

AIRFIELD NO 2

TURKEY KNOB

TACHIIWA
POINT

HIGASHI

AMPHITHEATER

**4th MARINE
DIVISION**

MINAMI

QUARRY

AIRFIELD NO 1

EAST BOAT BASIN

**1st MAR**

BLUE 2

BLUE 1

YELLOW 2

YELLOW 1

RED 2

*FUTATSU ROCK*

RED 1

GREEN

'MOUNT SURIBACHI'

*TOBIISHI POINT*

# IWO JIMA
# SHOWING KEY LOCATIONS
# 1st MARCH 1945

◇━━━━◇  Limit of Exploitation

▬▬▬▬▬  Divisional Boundary

The original caption to this image states: 'MOVING UP – The uniform of the Marines blends into the surrounding foliage as by ones and twos they struggle forward in the face of desperate Japanese fire during the battle for Volcano Island group stronghold, Iwo Jima.' Away from the beaches, the landscape of the island changed to scrubland. This proved of advantage to the defenders and an extreme disadvantage to the attackers. (USMC)

The original caption to this image states:'Battle for Iwo Jima, February–March 1945. Men of 'L' Company, 3rd Battalion, 21st Regiment moving forward under heavy mortar and machine gun fire in attempt to take #2 Airstrip. They have just relieved 4th Division. Photographed by Cpl. Page, February 24, 1945.' (USN)

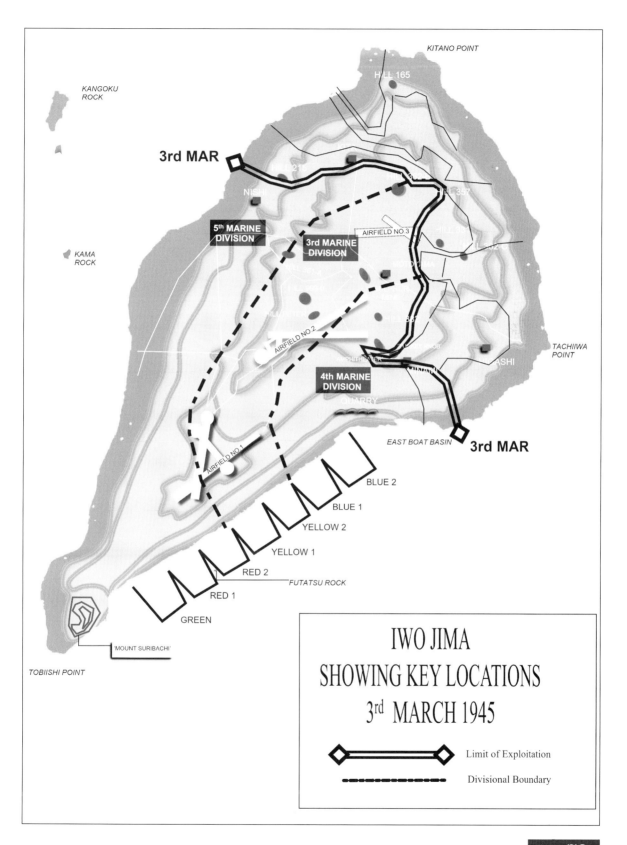

KITANO POINT

KANGOKU
ROCK

HILL 165

3rd MAR

NISHI

KAMA
ROCK

5th MARINE
DIVISION

3rd MARINE
DIVISION

HILL 357

AIRFIELD NO 3

4th MARINE
DIVISION

TACHIIWA
POINT

AMPHITHEATER

MINAMI

QUARRY

EAST BOAT BASIN

AIRFIELD NO.2

AIRFIELD NO.1

3rd MAR

BLUE 2

BLUE 1

YELLOW 2

YELLOW 1

RED 2

FUTATSU ROCK

RED 1

GREEN

'MOUNT SURIBACHI'

TOBIISHI POINT

IWO JIMA
SHOWING KEY LOCATIONS
3rd MARCH 1945

◇——————◇   Limit of Exploitation

■—■—■—■—■—■—■   Divisional Boundary

79

The original caption to this image states: 'Battle for Iwo Jima, February–March 1945. A Marine raises up in his hole and fires at a Japanese he has spotted during an advance. Photographed by Sgt Dreyfuss, March 11, 1945.' This image shows the difference in terrain encountered by the Marines as they advanced into the island's interior, this rocky terrain making another naturally defensive barrier. (USN)

The part of the operation conducted in the northern end of the island was much harder than the campaign for Suribachi. The terrain features were difficult, and the enemy was 'dug in' better. The defense he had was better concealed and harder to knock out due to there being piles of stone and small holes cut down into the stone, all being well concealed. Then in addition the ground was undermined with many caves and tunnels. These could not be bypassed but had to be left under guard and blown shut with demolitions, which, due to the number of men available for this work, slowed the operation … The fighting in the northern end was very discouraging. Troops were so close to the enemy positions that supporting weapons, even 60mm mortars, could not be used with safety. Yet the enemy was so well concealed that he could not be seen. The fire received was close and extremely accurate.

*After Action Report, 3rd Battalion, 28th Marines*

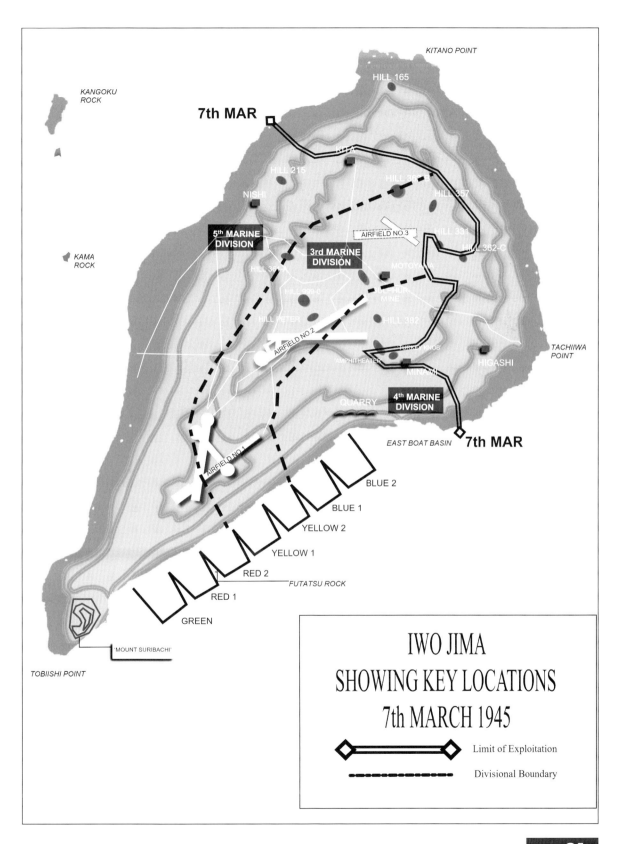

IWO JIMA
SHOWING KEY LOCATIONS
7th MARCH 1945

◇━━━━◇ Limit of Exploitation

●━━━━● Divisional Boundary

The original caption to this image states: 'Battle for Iwo Jima, February–March 1945. A tank dozer comes up, clearing the road as it comes. Photographed by Sgt Dreyfuss, March 9, 1945.' The dozer attachment for the Sherman tank was originally designed for clearing mines, overcoming ditches, craters, and other anti-tank obstacles. Working with the Caterpillar Tractor Company and two industrial producers of tractor blades, the LeTourneau and LaPlant-Choate companies, the US Army developed the blade for mine removal. Both tank dozer blades were approved for the Army's M4 Sherman medium tanks. The LeTourneau blade was cable-operated and the LaPlant-Choate system used a hydraulically operated blade. The driver could jettison the blade within ten seconds in case of emergency. (USN)

The original caption to this image states: 'BATTLE OF THE ROCKS – In a quarry-like ravine on the northern ridges of Iwo Jima, Marines use high explosives to blast the Japs. The thirst-crazed enemy remnants apparently are determined to resist to the end from well-defended positions in the honeycombed caves of these ridges.' The northern end of the island was extremely rugged volcanic terrain, often strong with the smell of sulphur fumes. (USMC)

In the final defensive area north of Nishi the increased natural defensive strength of the ground and the subterranean defensive features compensated for the reduced amounts of concrete and steel used by the Japanese .... Volcanic eruption has littered the whole northern end of the island with outcrops of sandstone and loose rock. The sandstone outcrops make cave digging easy for the japs ... Our troops obtained cover only by defilade or by piling loose rocks on the surface to form rock-reveted positions. A series of irregularly eroded, crisscrossed gorges with precipitous sides resulted in a series of compartments of various shapes. These were usually small but were lined with a labyrinth of natural and artificial caves which covered the approaches from all directions. Fields of fire were usually limited to 25 yards and an unusual characteristic of the Japanese defensive positions in this area was that the reverse slopes were as strongly fortified as were the forward slopes.

*5th Marine Division Intelligence Report*

The original caption to this image states: 'DIG IN AND DIG 'EM OUT – Along these rocky ridges and hills, the Marines waged a battle of numerous skirmishes against the enemy on Iwo Jima. Honey-combed with caves, the terrain was held by isolated units of the Japs who had to be dug out of the caves before the Marines could advance.' A Marine machine gun team dug in. Two M1 carbines are stacked ready for use, one of which has a grenade launcher fitted. Their .30 calibre M1917A1 machine gun is positioned in the lip of the dugout. (USMC)

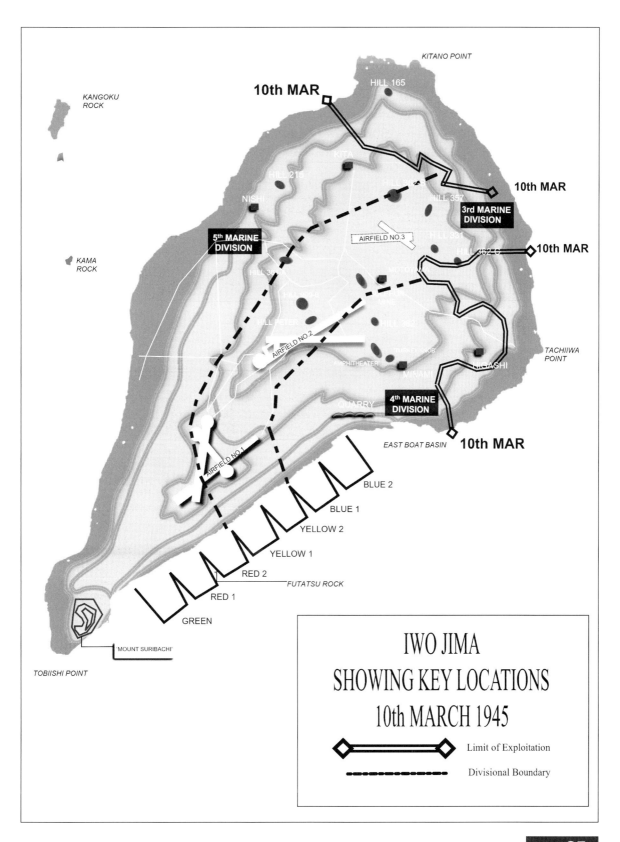

IWO JIMA
SHOWING KEY LOCATIONS
10th MARCH 1945

Limit of Exploitation

Divisional Boundary

85

This group of Marines surrounded by their equipment are pictured resting in a large shell crater which has been reinforced by sandbags. Resting, eating, reading letters from home, having a smoke. Typically what soldiers do when given a brief respite from battle. (USMC)

In attacking these positions, no Japanese were to be seen, in caves or crevices in the rocks, and as to give an all-around interlocking, ghost-like defense to each small compartment. Attacking troops were subjected to fire from the flanks and rear more than from their front. It was always difficult and often impossible to locate where defensive fires originated. The field of fire of the individual Japanese defender in his cave was often limited to an arc of 10 degrees or less; conversely, he was protected from fire except that coming back on this arc. The Japanese smokeless, flashless powder for small arms was of particular use here.

*5th Marine Division Intelligence Report*

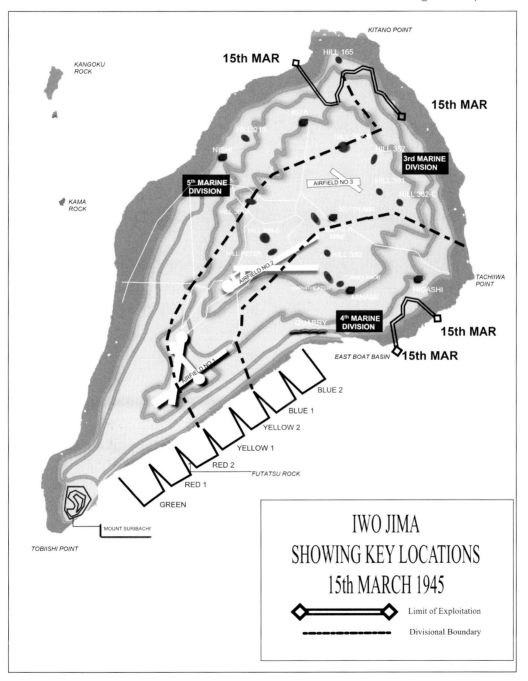

IWO JIMA
SHOWING KEY LOCATIONS
15th MARCH 1945

◇━━━◇  Limit of Exploitation

▬▬▬▬▬  Divisional Boundary

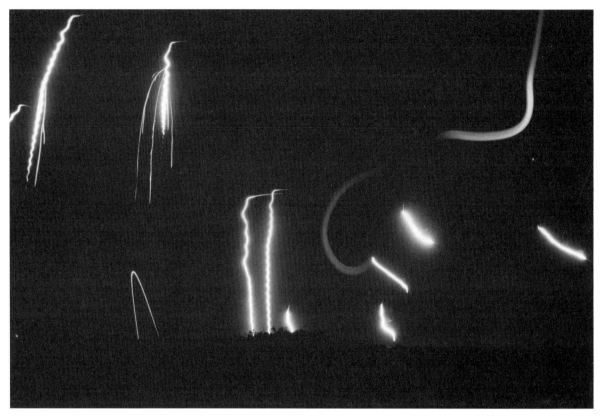

The original caption to this image states: 'STAR SHELLS OVER IWO – Illuminating shells fired from supporting warships light up the dark no-man's-land between the Japs and the front lines of the Third Marine Division on Iwo Jima. The lights were parachuted in from the sea every few minutes to prevent enemy infiltration.' The nights on Iwo Jima brought danger from Japanese infiltrators. Unable to move by daylight, the Japanese defenders came out at night not only to attack, but as the battle wore on to forage for food and water as their supplies ran out. At night a dangerous and surreal atmosphere pervaded. (USMC)

We all expected—maybe because of Hollywood movies showing battlefields quiet at night—that darkness would bring some relief from the shelling. Instead, our area received a steady sprinkling of random individual bursts all night long, interspersed at odd times with very intense combined artillery and mortar barrages. Even if nothing hit you, the continual shelling was just often enough and random enough to jar you awake (if you had been lucky enough to begin to doze).

In addition to explosive shells, both sides fired parachute flares all night long, trying to see what was going on. At times there were so many flares in the air that it looked like daylight—but they had a greenish cast which gave a very eerie look to an already chaotic landscape.

*Private First Class Howard N. McLaughlin Jr, USMCR, 5th Marine Division*

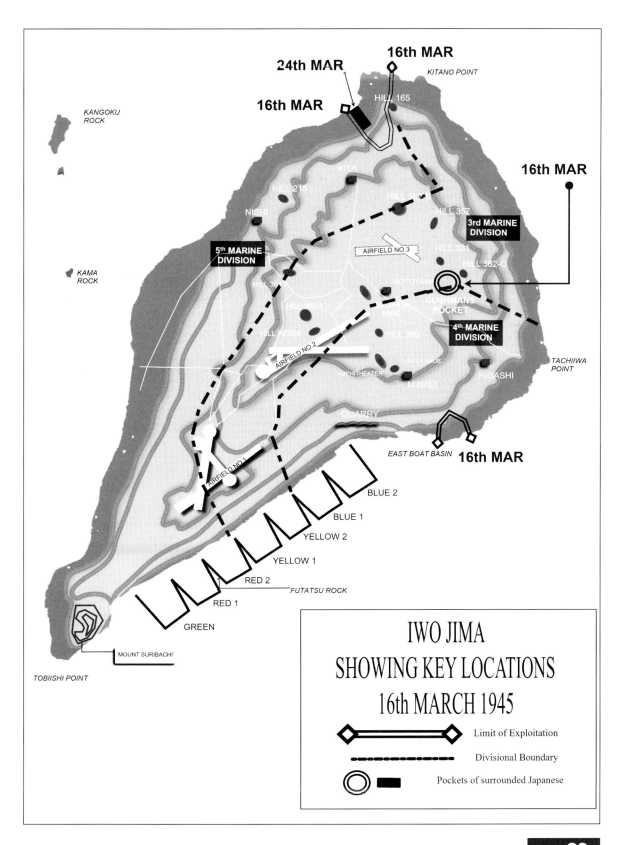

24th MAR
16th MAR
16th MAR

KITANO POINT
HILL 165

KANGOKU
ROCK

16th MAR

KITA
HILL 215

NISHI

HILL 357
3rd MARINE
DIVISION

AIRFIELD NO.3

HILL 331

5th MARINE
DIVISION

HILL 362-C
MOTOYAMA
CUSHMANS
POCKET

KAMA
ROCK

HILL 362

4th MARINE
DIVISION

HILL PETER
AIRFIELD NO 2

TACHIIWA
POINT

TURKEY KNOB
AMPHITHEATER
MINAMI
HIGASHI

QUARRY

EAST BOAT BASIN
16th MAR

AIRFIELD NO.1

BLUE 2

BLUE 1

YELLOW 2

YELLOW 1

RED 2
FUTATSU ROCK

RED 1

GREEN

'MOUNT SURIBACHI'

TOBIISHI POINT

## IWO JIMA
## SHOWING KEY LOCATIONS
## 16th MARCH 1945

◇━━━━━◇  Limit of Exploitation

▰▰▰▰▰  Divisional Boundary

◎  ▬  Pockets of surrounded Japanese

Whilst the island was officially declared secure on 16 March, the fighting continued until the end of March until all the main pockets of Japanese resistance were destroyed. Individual Japanese soldiers continued to fight on for some considerable time. The Marines had to continue to deal with these Japanese, as did the 147th Infantry Regiment who arrived at the end of May as the island garrison force. (USMC)

The thoughts of Corporal William W. Byrd (CT 28, 5th Marine Division) on the morning of 26 March perhaps sum up the thoughts of many of the Marines as they withdrew to the beach in preparation for leaving the island:

Martin Anderson from Salt Lake City and I walked up a hill and looked out across the vast Pacific Ocean. We looked to the north in the direction of Japan and wondered what lay ahead. We shook hands, and he said, 'Man, you need a shave.' Lieutenant Armstrong sent word to the other two companies in the 2nd Battalion that he had gotten word from the Command Post of the 28th Regiment to have our troops move out in about an hour. We were headed for the beach area near Mt. Suribachi, four miles away … Everyone got their gear together. My rifle was just about all I had. Lieutenant [Edwin] Armstrong looked around and was worried that some of the weary, dirty, twice-wounded Marines might not be able to make the hike. We formed two lines for our march back to the south end where we first landed thirty-six days earlier. As we walked down the single-lane road parallel to the beach, it seemed that everybody was looking down and not looking to the left, at all the hellish places where so many of our comrades had died.

## Congressional Medal of Honor Awards
### 19 February to 26 March 1945

Focusing on those who win bravery awards may seem to ignore the many men who quite likely never received recognition for deeds of equal bravery, but whose stories for various reasons were never recorded. As such, the citations provide valuable historical context and are a tribute not only to those who won them but to the many who did not. Twenty-one awards of the Congressional Medal of Honor were made for actions on Iwo Jima over the period 19 February to March 26. Nine were awarded posthumously. The details of each award are listed here in an approximate chronological sequence. The medal citations provide a direct narrative to the story and are representative in detail of those who won them and of their colleagues who served with them. They make inspiring reading.

Colonel Justice M. Chambers. USMCR, 3rd Assault Battalion Landing Team. 25th Marines, 4th Marine Division:

> For conspicuous gallantry and intrepidity at the risk of his life above and beyond the call of duty as commanding officer of the 3rd Assault Battalion Landing Team, 25th Marines, 4th Marine Division, in action against enemy Japanese forces on Iwo Jima, Volcano Islands, from 19 to 22 February 1945. Under a furious barrage of enemy machinegun and small-arms fire from the commanding cliffs on the right, Col. Chambers (then Lieutenant Col.) landed immediately after the initial assault waves of his battalion on D-day to find the momentum of the assault  threatened by heavy casualties from withering Japanese artillery, mortar rocket, machinegun, and rifle fire. Exposed to relentless hostile fire, he coolly

reorganized his battle-weary men, inspiring them to heroic efforts by his own valour and leading them in an attack on the critical, impregnable high ground from which the enemy was pouring an increasing volume of fire directly onto troops ashore as well as amphibious craft in succeeding waves. Constantly in the front lines encouraging his men to push forward against the enemy's savage resistance, Col. Chambers led the 8-hour battle to carry the flanking ridge top and reduce the enemy's fields of aimed fire, thus protecting the vital foothold gained. In constant defiance of hostile fire while reconnoitering the entire regimental combat team zone of action, he maintained contact with adjacent units and forwarded vital information to the regimental commander. His zealous fighting spirit undiminished despite terrific casualties and the loss of most of his key officers, he again reorganized his troops for renewed attack against the enemy's main line of resistance and was directing the fire of the rocket platoon when he fell, critically wounded. Evacuated under heavy Japanese fire, Col. Chambers, by forceful leadership, courage, and fortitude in the face of staggering odds, was directly instrumental in insuring the success of subsequent operations of the 5th Amphibious Corps on Iwo Jima, thereby sustaining and enhancing the finest traditions of the U.S. Naval Service.

Private First Class Jacklyn Harold Lucas, USMCR, 1st Battalion, 26th Marines, 5th Marine Division:

For conspicuous gallantry and intrepidity at the risk of his life above and beyond the call of duty while serving with the 1st Battalion, 26th Marines, 5th Marine Division, during action against enemy Japanese forces on Iwo Jima, Volcano Islands, 20 February 1945. While creeping through a treacherous, twisting ravine which ran in close proximity to a fluid and uncertain frontline on D-plus-1 day, PFC. Lucas and 3 other men were suddenly ambushed by a hostile patrol which savagely attacked with rifle fire and grenades. Quick to act when the lives of the small group were endangered by 2 grenades which landed directly in front of them, PFC. Lucas unhesitatingly hurled himself over his comrades upon one grenade and pulled the other under him, absorbing the whole blasting forces of the explosions in his own body in order to shield his companions from the concussion and murderous flying fragments. By his inspiring action and valiant spirit of self-sacrifice, he not only protected his comrades from certain injury or possible death but also enabled them to rout the Japanese patrol and continue the advance. His exceptionally courageous initiative and loyalty reflect the highest credit upon PFC. Lucas and the U.S. Naval Service.

Private First Class Donald Jack Ruhl, U.S. Marine Corps Reserve, Company E, 28th Marines, 5th Marine Division. Citation:

For conspicuous gallantry and intrepidity at the risk of his life above and beyond the call of duty while serving as a rifleman in an assault platoon of Company E, 28th Marines, 5th Marine Division, in action against enemy Japanese forces on Iwo Jima, Volcano Islands, from 19 to 21 February 1945. Quick to press the advantage after 8 Japanese had been driven from a blockhouse on D-day, PFC. Ruhl single-handedly attacked the group, killing 1 of the enemy with his bayonet and another by rifle fire in his determined attempt to annihilate the escaping troops. Cool and undaunted as the fury of hostile resistance steadily increased throughout the night, he voluntarily left the shelter of his tank trap early in the morning of D-day plus 1 and moved out under a tremendous volume of mortar and machinegun fire to rescue a wounded marine lying in an exposed position approximately 40 yards forward of the line. Half pulling and half carrying the wounded man, he removed him to a defiladed position, called for an assistant and a stretcher and, again running the gauntlet of hostile fire, carried the casualty to an aid station some 300 yards distant on the beach. Returning to his platoon, he continued his valiant efforts, volunteering to investigate an apparently abandoned Japanese gun emplacement 75 yards forward of the right flank during consolidation of the front lines, and subsequently occupying the position through the night to prevent the enemy from repossessing the valuable weapon. Pushing forward in the assault against the vast network of fortifications surrounding Mt. Suribachi the following morning, he crawled with his platoon guide to the top of a Japanese bunker to bring fire to bear on enemy troops located on the far side of the bunker. Suddenly a hostile grenade landed between the 2 Marines. Instantly PFC. Ruhl called a warning to his fellow marine and dived on the deadly missile, absorbing the full impact of the shattering explosion in his own body and protecting all within range from the danger of flying fragments although he might easily have dropped from his position on the edge of the bunker to the ground below. An indomitable fighter, PFC. Ruhl rendered heroic service toward the defeat of a ruthless enemy, and his valor, initiative and unfaltering spirit of self-sacrifice in the face of almost certain death sustain and enhance the highest traditions of the U.S. Naval Service. He gallantly gave his life for his country.

Private First Class Ruhl is buried in the Donald J. Ruhl Memorial Cemetery in Greybull, Wyoming.

Captain Hugo Robert Dunlap, USMCR, Company C, 1st Battalion, 26th Marines, 5th Marine Division:

For conspicuous gallantry and intrepidity at the risk of his life above and beyond the call of duty as commanding officer of Company C, 1st Battalion, 26th Marines, 5th Marine Division, in action against enemy Japanese forces during the seizure of Iwo Jima in the Volcano Islands, on 20 and 21 February, 1945. Defying uninterrupted blasts of Japanese artillery. mortar, rifle and machinegun fire, Capt. Dunlap led his troops in a determined advance from low ground uphill toward the steep cliffs from which the enemy poured a devastating rain of shrapnel and bullets, steadily inching forward until the tremendous volume of enemy fire from the caves located high to his front temporarily halted his progress. Determined not to yield, he crawled alone approximately 200 yards forward of his front lines, took observation at the base of the cliff 50 yards from Japanese lines, located the enemy gun positions and returned to his own lines where he relayed the vital information to supporting artillery and naval gunfire units. Persistently disregarding his own personal safety, he then placed himself in an exposed vantage point to direct more accurately the supporting fire and, working without respite for 2 days and 2 nights under constant enemy fire, skilfully directed a smashing bombardment against the almost impregnable Japanese positions despite numerous obstacles and heavy marine casualties. A brilliant leader, Capt. Dunlap inspired his men to heroic efforts during this critical phase of the battle and by his cool decision, indomitable fighting spirit, and daring tactics in the face of fanatic opposition greatly accelerated the final decisive defeat of Japanese countermeasures in his sector and materially furthered the continued advance of his company. His great personal valor and gallant spirit of self-sacrifice throughout the bitter hostilities reflect the highest credit upon Capt. Dunlap and the U.S. Naval Service.

Sergeant Franklin Ross Gray, USMCR, Company A, 1st Battalion, 25th Marines, 4th Marine Division:

For conspicuous gallantry and intrepidity at the risk of his life above and beyond the call of duty as a Platoon Sergeant attached to Company A, 1st Battalion, 25th Marines, 4th Marine Division, in action against enemy Japanese forces on Iwo Jima, Volcano Islands, 21 February 1945. Shrewdly gauging the tactical situation when his platoon was held up by a sudden barrage of hostile grenades while advancing toward the high ground northeast of Airfield No. 1, Sgt. Gray promptly organized the withdrawal of his men from enemy grenade range, quickly moved forward alone to reconnoiter and discovered a heavily mined area extending along the front of a strong network of emplacements joined by covered trenches. Although assailed by furious gunfire, he cleared a path leading through the minefield to one of the fortifications, then returned to the platoon position and, informing his leader of the serious situation, volunteered to initiate an attack under cover of 3 fellow Marines. Alone and unarmed but carrying a huge satchel charge, he crept up on the Japanese emplacement, boldly hurled the short-fused explosive and sealed the entrance. Instantly taken under machinegun fire from a second entrance to the same position, he unhesitatingly braved the increasingly vicious fusillades to crawl back for another charge, returned to his objective and blasted the second opening, thereby demolishing the position. Repeatedly covering the ground between the savagely defended enemy fortifications and his platoon area, he systematically approached, attacked and withdrew under blanketing fire to destroy a total of 6 Japanese positions, more than 25 troops and a quantity of vital ordnance gear and ammunition. Stout-hearted and indomitable, Sgt. Gray had single-handedly overcome a strong enemy garrison and had completely disarmed a large minefield before finally re-joining his unit. By his great personal valour, daring tactics and tenacious perseverance in the face of extreme peril, he had contributed materially to the fulfilment of his company mission. His gallant conduct throughout enhanced and sustained the highest traditions of the U.S. Naval Service.

Captain Joseph Jeremiah McCarthy, USMCR, 2nd Battalion, 24th Marines, 4th Marine Division:

For conspicuous gallantry and intrepidity at the risk of his life above and beyond the call of duty as commanding officer of a rifle company attached to the 2nd Battalion, 24th Marines, 4th Marine Division, in action against enemy Japanese forces during the seizure of Iwo Jima, Volcano Islands, on 21 February 1945. Determined to break through the enemy's cross-island defenses, Capt. McCarthy acted on his own initiative when his company advance was held up by uninterrupted Japanese rifle, machinegun, and high-velocity 47mm. fire during the approach to Motoyama Airfield No. 2. Quickly organizing a demolitions and  flamethrower team to accompany his picked rifle squad, he fearlessly led the way across 75 yards of fire-swept ground, charged a heavily fortified pillbox on the ridge of the front and, personally hurling hand grenades into the emplacement as he directed the combined operations of his small assault group, completely destroyed the hostile installation. Spotting 2 Japanese soldiers attempting an escape from the shattered pillbox, he boldly stood upright in full view of the enemy and dispatched both troops before advancing to a second emplacement under greatly intensified fire and then blasted the strong fortifications with a well-planned demolitions attack. Subsequently entering the ruins, he found a Japanese taking aim at one of our men and, with alert presence of mind, jumped the enemy, disarmed and shot him with his own weapon. Then, intent on smashing through the narrow breach, he rallied the remainder of his company and pressed a full attack with furious aggressiveness until he had neutralized all resistance and captured the ridge. An inspiring leader and indomitable fighter, Capt. McCarthy consistently disregarded all personal danger during the fierce conflict and, by his brilliant professional skill, daring tactics, and tenacious perseverance in the face of overwhelming odds, contributed materially to the success of his division's operations against this savagely defended outpost of the Japanese Empire. His cool decision and outstanding valor reflect the highest credit upon Capt. McCarthy and enhance the finest traditions of the U.S. Naval Service.

Corporal Hershel Woodrow Williams, USMCR, 21st Marines, 3rd Marine Division:

For conspicuous gallantry and intrepidity at the risk of his life above and beyond the call of duty as demolition sergeant serving with the 21st Marines, 3rd Marine Division, in action against enemy Japanese forces on Iwo Jima, Volcano Islands, 23 February 1945. Quick to volunteer his services when our tanks were manoeuvring vainly to open a lane for the infantry through the network of reinforced concrete pillboxes, buried mines, and black volcanic sands, Cpl. Williams daringly went forward alone to attempt the reduction of devastating machinegun fire from the unyielding positions. Covered only by 4 riflemen, he fought  desperately for 4 hours under terrific enemy small-arms fire and repeatedly returned to his own lines to prepare demolition charges and obtain serviced flamethrowers, struggling back, frequently to the rear of hostile emplacements, to wipe out 1 position after another. On 1 occasion, he daringly mounted a pillbox to insert the nozzle of his flamethrower through the air vent, killing the occupants and silencing the gun; on another he grimly charged enemy riflemen who attempted to stop him with bayonets and destroyed them with a burst of flame from his weapon. His unyielding determination and extraordinary heroism in the face of ruthless enemy resistance were directly instrumental in neutralizing one of the most fanatically defended Japanese strong points encountered by his regiment and aided vitally in enabling his company to reach its objective. Cpl. Williams' aggressive fighting spirit and valiant devotion to duty throughout this fiercely contested action sustain and enhance the highest traditions of the U.S. Naval Service.

Private First Class Douglas Thomas Jacobsen, USMCR, 3rd Battalion, 23rd Marines, 4th Marine Division:

For conspicuous gallantry and intrepidity at the risk of his life above and beyond the call of duty while serving with the 3rd Battalion, 23rd Marines, 4th Marine Division, in combat against enemy Japanese forces during the seizure of Iwo Jima in the Volcano Island, 26 February 1945. Promptly destroying a stubborn 20mm. antiaircraft gun and its crew after assuming the duties of a bazooka man who had been killed, PFC. Jacobson waged a relentless battle as his unit fought desperately toward the summit of Hill 382 in an effort to penetrate the heart of Japanese cross-island defence. Employing his weapon with ready accuracy when his platoon was halted by overwhelming enemy fire on 26 February, he first destroyed 2 hostile machinegun positions, then attacked a large blockhouse, completely neutralizing the fortification before dispatching the 5-man crew of a second pillbox and exploding the installation with a terrific demolitions blast. Moving steadily forward, he wiped out an earth-covered rifle emplacement and, confronted by a cluster of similar emplacements which constituted the perimeter of enemy defences in his assigned sector, fearlessly advanced, quickly reduced all 6 positions to a shambles, killed 10 of the enemy, and enabled our forces to occupy the strong point. Determined to widen the breach thus forced, he volunteered his services to an adjacent assault company, neutralized a pillbox holding up its advance, opened fire on a Japanese tank pouring a steady stream of bullets on one of our supporting tanks, and smashed the enemy tank's gun turret in a brief but furious action culminating in a single-handed assault against still another blockhouse and the subsequent neutralization of its firepower. By his dauntless skill and valour, PFC. Jacobson destroyed a total of 16 enemy positions and annihilated approximately 75 Japanese, thereby contributing essentially to the success of his division's operations against this fanatically defended outpost of the Japanese Empire. His gallant conduct in the face of tremendous odds enhanced and sustained the highest traditions of the U.S. Naval Service.

Gunnery Sergeant Gary Willian Walsh, USMCR, Company G, 3rd Battalion, 27th Marines, 5th Marine Division:

For extraordinary gallantry and intrepidity at the risk of his life above and beyond the call of duty as leader of an assault platoon, attached to Company G, 3rd Battalion, 27th Marines, 5th Marine Division, in action against enemy Japanese forces at Iwo Jima, Volcano Islands on 27 February 1945. With the advance of his company toward Hill 362 disrupted by vicious machinegun fire from a forward position which guarded the approaches to this key enemy stronghold, G/Sgt. Walsh fearlessly charged at the head of his platoon against the Japanese entrenched on the ridge above him, utterly oblivious to the unrelenting fury of hostile automatic weapons fire and hand grenades employed with fanatic desperation to smash his daring assault. Thrown back by the enemy's savage resistance, he once again led his men in a seemingly impossible attack up the steep, rocky slope, boldly defiant of the annihilating streams of bullets which saturated the area. Despite his own casualty losses and the overwhelming advantage held by the Japanese in superior numbers and dominant position, he gained the ridge's top only to be subjected to an intense barrage of hand grenades thrown by the remaining Japanese staging a suicidal last stand on the reverse slope. When one of the grenades fell in the midst of his surviving men, huddled together in a small trench, G/Sgt. Walsh, in a final valiant act of complete self-sacrifice, instantly threw himself upon the deadly bomb, absorbing with his own body the full and terrific force of the explosion. Through his extraordinary initiative and inspiring valour in the face of almost certain death, he saved his comrades from injury and possible loss of life and enabled his company to seize and hold this vital enemy position. He gallantly gave his life for his country.

Gunnery Sergeant Walsh is buried in the Arlington National Cemetery.

Private Wilson Douglas Watson, USMCR, 2nd Battalion, 9th Marines, 3rd Marine Division:

For conspicuous gallantry and intrepidity at the risk of his life above and beyond the call of duty as automatic rifleman serving with the 2nd Battalion, 9th Marines, 3rd Marine Division, during action against enemy Japanese forces on Iwo Jima, Volcano Islands, 26 and 27 February 1945. With his squad abruptly halted by intense fire from enemy fortifications in the high rocky ridges and crags commanding the line of advance, Pvt. Watson boldly rushed 1 pillbox and fired into the embrasure with his weapon, keeping the enemy pinned down single-handedly until he was in a position to hurl in a grenade, and then running to the rear of the emplacement to destroy the retreating Japanese and enable his platoon to take its objective. Again pinned down at the foot of a small hill, he dauntlessly scaled the jagged incline under fierce mortar and machinegun barrages and, with his assistant BAR man, charged the crest of the hill, firing from his hip. Fighting furiously against Japanese troops attacking with grenades and knee mortars from the reverse slope, he stood fearlessly erect in his exposed position to cover the hostile entrenchments and held the hill under savage fire for 15 minutes, killing 60 Japanese before his ammunition was exhausted and his platoon was able to join him. His courageous initiative and valiant fighting spirit against devastating odds were directly responsible for the continued advance of his platoon, and his inspiring leadership throughout this bitterly fought action reflects the highest credit upon Pvt. Watson and the U.S. Naval Service.

Corporal Charles Joseph Berry, U.S. Marine Corps, 1st Battalion, 26th Marines, 5th Marine Division:

For conspicuous gallantry and intrepidity at the risk of his life above and beyond the call of duty as member of a machinegun crew, serving with the 1st Battalion, 26th Marines, 5th Marine Division, in action against enemy Japanese forces during the seizure of Iwo Jima in the Volcano Islands, on 3 March 1945. Stationed in the front lines, Cpl. Berry manned his weapon with alert readiness as he maintained a constant vigil with other members of his gun crew during the hazardous night hours. When infiltrating Japanese soldiers launched a surprise attack  shortly after midnight in an attempt to overrun his position, he engaged in a pitched hand grenade duel, returning the dangerous weapons with prompt and deadly accuracy until an enemy grenade landed in the foxhole. Determined to save his comrades, he unhesitatingly chose to sacrifice himself and immediately dived on the deadly missile, absorbing the shattering violence of the exploding charge in his own body and protecting the others from serious injury. Stout hearted and indomitable, Cpl. Berry fearlessly yielded his own life that his fellow Marines might carry on the relentless battle against a ruthless enemy and his superb valor and unfaltering devotion to duty in the face of certain death reflect the highest credit upon himself and upon the U.S. Naval Service. He gallantly gave his life for his country.

Corporal Berry is buried in Elmwood Cemetery, Lorain, Lorain County, Ohio.

Private First Class William Robert Caddy, USMCR, Company I, 3rd Battalion, 26th Marines, 5th Marine Division:

For conspicuous gallantry and intrepidity at the risk of his life above and beyond the call of duty while serving as a rifleman with Company I, 3rd Battalion, 26th Marines, 5th Marine Division, in action against enemy Japanese forces during the seizure of Iwo Jima in the Volcano Islands, 3 March 1945. Consistently aggressive, PFC. Caddy boldly defied shattering Japanese machinegun and small arms fire to move forward with his platoon leader and another marine during the determined advance of his company through an isolated sector and, gaining the comparative safety of a shell hole, took temporary cover with his comrades. Immediately pinned down by deadly sniper fire from a well-concealed position, he made several unsuccessful attempts to again move forward and then, joined by his platoon leader, engaged the enemy in a fierce exchange of hand grenades until a Japanese grenade fell beyond reach in the shell hole. Fearlessly disregarding all personal danger, PFC. Caddy instantly dived on the deadly missile, absorbing the exploding charge in his own body and protecting the others from serious injury. Stout-hearted and indomitable, he unhesitatingly yielded his own life that his fellow Marines might carry on the relentless battle against a fanatic enemy. His dauntless courage and valiant spirit of self-sacrifice in the face of certain death reflect the highest credit upon PFC. Caddy and upon the U.S. Naval Service. He gallantly gave his life for his comrades.

Private First Class Caddy is buried in the U.S. National Memorial Cemetery of the Pacific in Honolulu, Hawaii.

Sergeant William George Harrell, U.S. Marine Corps, 1st Battalion, 28th Marines, 5th Marine Division:

For conspicuous gallantry and intrepidity at the risk of his life above and beyond the call of duty as leader of an assault group attached to the 1st Battalion, 28th Marines, 5th Marine Division during hand-to-hand combat with enemy Japanese at Iwo Jima, Volcano Islands, on 3 March 1945. Standing watch alternately with another marine in a terrain studded with caves and ravines, Sgt. Harrell was holding a position in a perimeter defence around the company command post when Japanese troops infiltrated our lines in the early hours of dawn. Awakened by a sudden attack, he quickly opened fire with his carbine and killed 2 of the enemy as they emerged from a ravine in the light of a star shell-burst. Unmindful of his danger as hostile grenades fell closer, he waged a fierce lone battle until an exploding missile tore off his left hand and fractured his thigh. He was vainly attempting to reload the carbine when his companion returned from the command post with another weapon. Wounded again by a Japanese who rushed the foxhole wielding a saber in the darkness, Sgt. Harrell succeeded in drawing his pistol and killing his opponent and then ordered his wounded companion to a place of safety. Exhausted by profuse bleeding but still unbeaten, he fearlessly met the challenge of 2 more enemy troops who charged his position and placed a grenade near his head. Killing 1 man with his pistol, he grasped the sputtering grenade with his good right hand, and, pushing it painfully toward the crouching soldier, saw his remaining assailant destroyed but his own hand severed in the explosion. At dawn Sgt. Harrell was evacuated from a position hedged by the bodies of 12 dead Japanese, at least 5 of whom he had personally destroyed in his self-sacrificing defense of the command post. His grim fortitude, exceptional valor, and indomitable fighting spirit against almost insurmountable odds reflect the highest credit upon himself and enhance the finest traditions of the U.S. Naval Service.

Second Lieutenant John Harold Leims, USMCR, Company B, 1st Battalion, 9th Marines, 3rd Marine Division:

For conspicuous gallantry and intrepidity at the risk of his life above and beyond the call of duty as commanding officer of Company B, 1st Battalion, 9th Marines, 3rd Marine Division, in action against enemy Japanese forces on Iwo Jima in the Volcano Islands, 7 March 1945. Launching a surprise attack against the rock-imbedded fortification of a dominating Japanese hill position, 2nd Lieutenant Leims spurred his company forward with indomitable determination and, skilfully directing his assault platoons against the cave-emplaced enemy troops and heavily fortified pillboxes, succeeded in capturing the objective in later afternoon. When it became apparent that his assault platoons were cut off in this newly won position, approximately 400 yards forward of adjacent units and lacked all communication with the command post, he personally advanced and laid telephone lines across the isolating expanse of open fire-swept terrain. Ordered to withdraw his command after he had joined his forward platoons, he immediately complied, adroitly effecting the withdrawal of his troops without incident. Upon arriving at the rear, he was informed that several casualties had been left at the abandoned ridge position beyond the frontlines. Although suffering acutely from the strain and exhaustion of battle, he instantly went forward despite darkness and the slashing fury of hostile machinegun fire, located and carried to safety one seriously wounded marine and then, running the gauntlet of enemy fire for the third time that night, again made his tortuous way into the bullet-riddled death-trap and rescued another of his wounded men. A dauntless leader, concerned at all time for the welfare of his men, 2nd Lieutenant Leims soundly maintained the coordinated strength of his battle-wearied company under extremely difficult conditions and, by his bold tactics, sustained aggressiveness, and heroic disregard for all personal danger, contributed essentially to the success of his division's operations against this vital Japanese base. His valiant conduct in the face of fanatic opposition sustains and enhances the highest traditions of the U.S. Naval Service.

Private First Class James Dennis La Belle, USMCR, 27th Marines, 5th Marine Division:

For conspicuous gallantry and intrepidity at the risk of his life above and beyond the call of duty while attached to the 27th Marines, 5th Marine Division, in action against enemy Japanese forces during the seizure of Iwo Jima in the Volcano Islands, 8 March 1945. Filling a gap in the front lines during a critical phase of the battle, PFC. LaBelle had dug into a foxhole with 2 other Marines and, grimly aware of the enemy's persistent attempts to blast a way through our lines with hand grenades, applied himself with steady concentration to maintaining a sharply vigilant watch during the hazardous night hours. Suddenly a hostile grenade landed beyond reach in his foxhole. Quickly estimating the situation, he determined to save the others if possible, shouted a warning, and instantly dived on the deadly missile, absorbing the exploding charge in his own body and thereby protecting his comrades from serious injury. Stout hearted and indomitable, he had unhesitatingly relinquished his own chance of survival that his fellow Marines might carry on the relentless fight against a fanatic enemy

His dauntless courage, cool decision and valiant spirit of self-sacrifice in the face of certain death reflect the highest credit upon PFC. LaBelle and upon the U.S. Naval Service. He gallantly gave his life in the service of his country.

Private First Class La Belle is buried in Fort Snelling National Cemetery, Minneapolis, Hennepin County, Minnesota.

First Lieutenant Jack Lummus, USMCR, 2nd Battalion, 27th Marines, 5th Marine Division:

For conspicuous gallantry and intrepidity at the risk of his life above and beyond the call of duty as leader of a Rifle Platoon attached to the 2nd Battalion, 27th Marines, 5th Marine Division, in action against enemy Japanese forces on Iwo Jima in the Volcano Islands, 8 March 1945. Resuming his assault tactics with bold decision after fighting without respite for 2 days and nights, 1st Lieutenant Lummus slowly advanced his platoon against an enemy deeply entrenched in a network of mutually supporting positions. Suddenly halted by a terrific concentration of hostile fire, he unhesitatingly moved forward of his front lines in an effort to neutralize the Japanese position. Although knocked to the ground when an enemy grenade exploded close by, he immediately recovered himself and, again moving forward despite the intensified barrage, quickly located, attacked, and destroyed the occupied emplacement. Instantly taken under fire by the garrison of a supporting pillbox and further assailed by the slashing fury of hostile rifle fire, he fell under the impact of a second enemy grenade but, courageously disregarding painful shoulder wounds, staunchly continued his heroic one-man assault and charged the second pillbox, annihilating all the occupants. Subsequently returning to his platoon position, he fearlessly traversed his lines under fire, encouraging his men to advance and directing the fire of supporting tanks against other stubbornly holding Japanese emplacements. Held up again by a devastating barrage, he again moved into the open, rushed a third heavily fortified installation and killed the defending troops. Determined to crush all resistance, he led his men indomitably, personally attacking foxholes and spider traps with his carbine and systematically reducing the fanatic opposition until, stepping on a land mine, he sustained fatal wounds. By his outstanding valor, skilled tactics, and tenacious perseverance in the face of overwhelming odds, 1st Lieutenant Lummus had inspired his stout hearted Marines to continue the relentless drive northward, thereby contributing materially to the success of his regimental mission. His dauntless leadership and unwavering devotion to duty throughout sustain and enhance the highest traditions of the U.S. Naval Service. He gallantly gave his life in the service of his country.

First Lieutenant Lummus is buried in Myrtle Cemetery Ennis, Ellis County, Texas.

Platoon Sergeant Joseph Rodolph Julian, USMCR, 1st Battalion, 27th Marines, 5th Marine Division:

For conspicuous gallantry and intrepidity at the risk of his life above and beyond the call of duty as a P/Sgt. serving with the 1st Battalion, 27th Marines, 5th Marine Division, in action against enemy Japanese forces during the seizure of Iwo Jima in the Volcano Islands, 9 March 1945. Determined to force a breakthrough when Japanese troops occupying trenches and fortified positions on the left front laid down a terrific machinegun and mortar barrage in a desperate effort to halt his company's advance, P/Sgt. Julian quickly established his platoon's guns in strategic supporting positions, and then, acting on his own initiative, fearlessly moved forward to execute a one-man assault on the nearest pillbox. Advancing alone, he hurled deadly demolition and white phosphorus grenades into the emplacement, killing 2 of the enemy and driving the remaining 5 out into the adjoining trench system. Seizing a discarded rifle, he jumped into the trench and dispatched the 5 before they could make an escape. Intent on wiping out all resistance, he obtained more explosives and, accompanied by another marine, again charged the hostile fortifications and knocked out 2 more cave positions. Immediately thereafter, he launched a bazooka attack unassisted, firing 4 rounds into the 1 remaining pillbox and completely destroying it before he fell, mortally wounded by a vicious burst of enemy fire. Stout hearted and indomitable, P/Sgt. Julian consistently disregarded all personal danger and, by his bold decision, daring tactics, and relentless fighting spirit during a critical phase of the battle, contributed materially to the continued advance of his company and to the success of his division's operations in the sustained drive toward the conquest of this fiercely defended outpost of the Japanese Empire. His outstanding valor and unfaltering spirit of self-sacrifice throughout the bitter conflict sustained and enhanced the highest traditions of the U.S. Naval Service. He gallantly gave his life for his country.

Platoon Sergeant Julian is buried in the Long Island National Cemetery, East Farmingdale, Suffolk County, New York.

Private Franklin Earl Sigler, USMCR, 2nd Battalion, 26th Marines, 5th Marine Division:

For conspicuous gallantry and intrepidity at the risk of his life above and beyond the call of duty while serving with the 2nd Battalion, 26th Marines, 5th Marine Division, in action against enemy Japanese forces during the seizure of Iwo Jima in the Volcano Islands on 14 March 1945. Voluntarily taking command of his rifle squad when the leader became a casualty, Pvt. Sigler fearlessly led a bold charge against an enemy gun installation which had held up the advance of his company for several days and, reaching the position in advance of the others, assailed the emplacement with hand grenades and personally annihilated the entire crew. As additional Japanese troops opened fire from concealed tunnels and caves above, he quickly scaled the rocks leading to the attacking guns, surprised the enemy with a furious I-man assault and, although severely wounded in the encounter, deliberately crawled back to his squad position where he steadfastly refused evacuation, persistently directing heavy machinegun and rocket barrages on the Japanese cave entrances. Undaunted by the merciless rain of hostile fire during the intensified action, he gallantly disregarded his own painful wounds to aid casualties, carrying 3 wounded squad members to safety behind the lines and returning to continue the battle with renewed determination until ordered to retire for medical treatment. Stout hearted and indomitable in the face of extreme peril, Pvt. Sigler, by his alert initiative, unfaltering leadership, and daring tactics in a critical situation, effected the release of his besieged company from enemy fire and contributed essentially to its further advance against a savagely fighting enemy. His superb valor, resolute fortitude, and heroic spirit of self-sacrifice throughout reflect the highest credit upon Pvt. Sigler and the U.S. Naval Service.

Private George Phillips, 2nd Battalion, 28th Marines, 5th Marine Division, U.S. Marine Corps Reserve:

For conspicuous gallantry and intrepidity at the risk of his life above and beyond the call of duty while serving with the 2nd Battalion, 28th Marines, 5th Marine Division, in action against enemy Japanese forces during the seizure of Iwo Jima in the Volcano Islands, on 14 March 1945. Standing the foxhole watch while other members of his squad rested after a night of bitter hand grenade fighting against infiltrating Japanese troops, Pvt. Phillips was the only member of his unit alerted when an enemy hand grenade was tossed into their midst. Instantly shouting a warning, he unhesitatingly threw himself on the deadly missile, absorbing the shattering violence of the exploding charge in his own body and protecting his comrades from serious injury. Stout hearted and indomitable, Pvt. Phillips willingly yielded his own life that his fellow Marines might carry on the relentless battle against a fanatic enemy. His superb valor and unfaltering spirit of self-sacrifice in the face of certain death reflect the highest credit upon himself and upon the U.S. Naval Service. He gallantly gave his life for his country.

Private Phillips is buried in Bethel Cemetery, Labadie, Franklin County, Missouri.

# Chapter Eight

# Consolidation

One of the key elements of any military victory is the ability to supply troops with the equipment they need. This has to be provided at the right time, at the right place and in the right quantities. Logistics and administration are a key component, as are the men that support this vital lifeline. The amphibious operations in the Pacific required a particular type of logistic solution. At Iwo Jima, resupply for the troops ashore had to come across the landing beaches, as did the equipment to consolidate and build the airfields. The unloading conditions were impeded by the difficult nature of the beaches used for initial landings. For several days these were blocked by wreckage consisting of small boats, LVTs, tanks and vehicles. The beach clearance was made difficult by sporadic enemy mortar and artillery fire. At various times, moving equipment on shore had to be stopped as beaches were required to be closed due to surf conditions and shifting of the sand on the beach. Exits had to be created using bulldozers. In some instances, the careless loading of LSTs, LSMs, and LCTs from transports further retarded the discharge of supplies on the beach. Initially, only the western beaches were utilized for unloading. The situation was alleviated when the eastern beaches were eventually able to be used for offloading supplies. For the operations at Iwo Jima, special preloading of equipment and supplies ensured that a balanced supply of rations, fuels and ammunition were available to the assault troops. These supplies were loaded onto the decks of LSTs and were designed to provide priority items on D-Day plus one day. Thirty-eight LSTs were loaded accordingly at Pearl Harbor and sailed with the assaulting force. Some supplies were also able to be dropped by air.

As the attacking forces pushed inland, resupply and movement of equipment ramped up to meet the demand and to provide the necessary equipment to build the airfield.

The amphibious DUKW vehicles played a key part in the unloading of supplies. Five DUKW companies equipped with 250 vehicles supported the operation, with three of the five supplied by the US Army.

The official after-action report detailed the use of the DUKWs:

Men from a naval construction battalion (Seabees) unloading cargo from a DUKW onto black sand beaches at Iwo Jima during the invasion. The chaotic post-landing situation can be seen. (Seabee Archive)

All of the DUKWs found it difficult to beach without aid from tractors or winches from other vehicles. The steep beaches caused undue frequency of broaching. The front wheels upon hitting the beach were not capable of pulling the vehicles forward, and the rough sea continuously pounding the rear end of the DUKW eventually caused broaching. If a tractor with winch and sufficient power was not on the spot to pull the DUKWs on shore, the vehicle was turned over and pounded by the surf. Very few DUKWs landed in the assault area were hit by gun fire, although several were hit by sniper fire without the driver's knowledge and sank a short time after floating out to pick up additional cargo. Refuelling facilities as planned were on floating barges, however, the constantly increasing seas made refuelling difficult, causing the vehicle to pick up considerable water in the fuel tanks. Hand bilge pumas were effective when operated in time, or when the sea was not too rough. Several DUKWs were kept afloat and saved by hand bilge pumps, although many of the hand bilge pumps were damaged in transit on the crowded LSTs. The LSTs designated as repair ships for DUKWs moved from one area to another, and frequently a lame vehicle sank before it could reach the repair LST. The low visibility from a DUKW at sea made it difficult to locate or follow the LSTs. The LSTs did not permit welding on the well decks, and a large share of the DUKW maintenance failed to be accomplished because of this regulation. Several instances are reported where disabled DUKWs were being towed or aided by other DUKWs when both swamped and sunk. This occurred particularly on the night of D-Day.

The control centre would not permit disabled DUKWs to land on shore due to enemy fire, and unless aided by a tractor, lame DUKW could not clear the beaches. Several vehicles sunk, practically in reach of shore.

Several DUKWs were reported to have sunk as soon as they left the ramps of the LSTs. These sinkings are usually due to three causes:

(1) Overloading.
(2) Too rapid forward movement of the LST.
(3) Too rapid disembarking by the vehicle.

The quickest way to clear wrecked equipment from a section of the Iwo beachhead was to blast it away with demolition charges. (USMC)

Wrecked Marine Corps' landing boats on the beach. (USMC)

Marines unload supplies from an LSM that has dropped its ramp almost clear of the water to allow supplies to be rolled ashore for the inland drive, 22 February. (USMC)

The original caption to this image states: 'Marines Scouting Minefield on Beach, Iwo Jima, February 1945. TICKLISH TASK – Inch by inch, Marine demolition crews prod the ground with their bayonets to locate Japanese land mines on the Iwo Jima beachhead. After the taped-off area has been declared safe, supplies and equipment will be transported over this lane en route to the front lines.' Marine engineers took the initial responsibility for clearing access through minefields and marking unexploded ammunition. The Japanese had laid minefields and booby traps. Marine bomb disposal companies took over responsibility for clearing the beaches and hinterland once they had been captured. Initially LVTs were filled with unexploded ordnance, which was taken out to the sea approximately 750 to 1,000 yards from the beach and dumped into the sea. Numerous 'dud' projectiles of all sizes were found scattered along the beaches. Many of these had been previously marked by the divisional engineers. (USMC)

Armoured bulldozers such as this played a vital role in the capture of Iwo Jima. They worked clearing exits to the beach as bulldozers, as well as being used to seal in dug-in Japanese positions. This example is an International Harvester TD-9 dozer with Bucyrus-Erie blade as used by the US naval construction battalions.

The original caption to this image states: 'Iwo Jima February 1945. Supplies are unloaded from the vast fleet of ships offshore and ration dumps of the 3rd and 4th Marine Divisions are established on the beach.' This image shows part of the massive number of stores needed to supply the three Marine divisions and attached units. (USMC)

The original caption to this image states: 'Marines Stacking Supplies on Beach, Iwo Jima, February 1945. RATIONS – Marines stack their rations about 300 yards inland from the water's edge on the Iwo Jima beachhead.' (USMC)

One of the very unglamorous parts of being on the lines was that all supplies had to be carried up there on somebody's back. The terrain was generally too rugged for an amtrac, and even if the driver got up near the lines he would be such a target that he couldn't unload. So, the tractors stopped back a ways, in a sheltered area, and each box of ammo, rations, or grenades had to be manhandled forward, along with those five-gallon water cans with contents that tasted like gasoline, and even medical supplies. (This work was usually done at the end of the day's fighting—just when you were feeling your best.) Sometimes two or three men from the demolition squad aught have to spend a whole day crawling back and forth, bringing up more explosives.

*Private First Class Howard N. McLaughlin Jr, USMCR, 5th Marine Division*

The original caption to this image states: 'ALL ASHORE – The difficulties encountered in getting supplies ashore at Iwo Jima, and the valiant work of the shore parties, is graphically illustrated in this picture taken from the bow of a landing vessel. The Marines in this right foreground are supply parties preparing to tote critical materials to the front lines.' (USMC)

What it was all about – the B-29 airstrip under construction on Iwo Jima. Seabees from the 62nd NCB work around the clock to build the facility on 30 April. The tower in the foreground and others to the right were built for floodlights to allow work to continue at night. The Marine engineers and naval construction battalions commenced work on the airfield on 26 February and by 1 March had constructed a 3,800ft runway suitable for fighter aircraft operation, but still too short for B-29 bombers. (Seabee Archive)

The original caption to this image states: 'Marine "Water Boy", Iwo Jima, 1945 'MODERN "GUNGA DIN" – Iwo Japs made suicidal but futile attempts to raid life-giving water dumps like the one seen here. "Water boy" was a hazardous job in the early days of the battle as all water had to be brought ashore in cans and transported through heavy enemy fire to the front lines. Handling the distribution are, (left to right): Marine Quartermaster Sergeant Frank Writter, of Philadelphia, Pa., and Sergeant Edward M. Lipski, of Mt. Thom, Mass.' Water on Iwo Jima had always been in short supply, and this had been a particular problem for the Japanese defenders. Providing drinking water for the attacking Marines required special provision using distillation plants. Accordingly, sea water provided the only practical source of water supply. (USMC)

The original caption to this image states: 'Work on Motoyama Airfield, Iwo Jima, 1945. UNDER CONSTRUCTION – Having pushed the Japs back from Motoyama Airfield Number One, the U.S. Marines commence immediate construction work on the Iwo Jima bomber strip. In the background is Mt. Suribachi, volcano mountain at the tip of the island.' It was necessary to clear the existing runway and improve the landing facilities as quickly as possible to not only keep it open for emergency landings by support and observation aircraft, but to ready it for its primary purpose – enabling damaged aircraft or aircraft short of fuel conducting bombing missions on the Japanese mainland to land on the island. (USMC)

The original caption to this image states: 'Work on Motoyama Airfield, Iwo Jima, 1945. PREPARING IT – Preparing the field for immediate use by American planes, Jap equipment is used on the former enemy Motoyama airfield Number One on Iwo Jima, where the Marines seized an island only 675 statute miles from the Jap home islands.' (USMC)

The original caption to this image states: 'Work on Motoyama Airfield, Iwo Jima, 1945. WORK – While Mount Suribachi frowns down upon them, U.S. Marines, before the battle for Iwo Jima has hardly more than cleared Motoyama Number One Airfield, commence reconstruction work on the field.' (USMC)

The original caption to this image states: 'Motoyama Airfield, Iwo Jima, 1945. ANOTHER AIRFIELD – Motoyama Airfield Number One on Iwo Jima is not Marine Corps property, having fallen to the Leathernecks when they invaded the Volcano group island. Work is in progress on the field.' (USMC)

The original caption to this image states: 'Arrival of Mail to Iwo Jima, 1945. AIR MAIL SPECIAL – Jubilant Marines gather parapacks of mail dropped by a transport plane for Leatherneck troops on the American-held portion of Iwo Jima. The Air Delivery Section of the V Amphibious Corps was set up at the 7th Field Depot on Saipan. Emergency supplies not readily available were delivered by air.'

The use of supply by air during the operation was deemed to be a great success. It was recorded that no more than fifteen rounds of 81mm ammunition were damaged as a result of being dropped by air supply. This was particularly creditable as the men who received the drops had no previous experience or training with this type of work. (USMC)

# Chapter Nine

# The Human Cost

The bitter and protracted fighting that took place during the assault on Iwo Jima resulted in 17,319 men being wounded. They were treated by their colleagues, corpsmen and doctors, and a stream of wounded men passed along the chain of evacuation to receive medical attention. Those wounded requiring evacuation were embarked on hospital ships and LSTs lying offshore. Initially, casualties were carried from the beach to LST(J)s in landing craft, LVTs, and DUKWs, but when surf conditions became too bad, small landing craft could no longer approach the beaches and only amphibious vehicles (DUKWs & LVTs) could be used. The wounded were evacuated to three hospital ships, AH *Solace*, AH *Samaritan* and AH *Bountiful*, along with four hospital LSTs. Together with departing transports, these ships evacuated a total of 13,737 casualties from Iwo Jima. The *Solace* and *Samaritan* made turn around trips from the target area to the Marianas.

Space on Iwo Jima was at a premium and medical units had to compete with everyone else for places to set up their facilities. Disused Japanese airplane revetments, trenches, empty water cisterns and bunkers were converted for medical use. Portable operating rooms were set up – sometimes in craters covered with tarpaulins to keep out dust and cold. Medical personnel serving with front-line units and beach evacuation stations were also amongst the casualties. Subjected to intense enemy fire as they moved about caring for the wounded, they were frequently deliberately targeted and shot alongside men they sought to help. Acts of heroism and self-sacrifice were common among these men as they worked tirelessly to administer first aid. Casualties among doctors and corpsmen totalled 738, including 197 killed.

The V Amphibious Corps after-action report, signed by its Commanding Officer Major General H. Schmidt, concluded:

> This operation was conducted against a heavily fortified position in which there was little choice as to where to land. It was not practicable to go around. The cost of the operation was heavy, but the present use of this base indicates that it was worth the cost. Some reduction in the number of casualties might have been affected by a more deliberate conduct of the attack and increased

preparations prior to the day-to-day assaults, but time was considered to be an important factor. Other operations were pending, which required utilization of elements released from this operation. Also, the position was exposed and there was a constant hazard of strong enemy air attacks on shipping and shore facilities at the target. These factors all indicated the necessity for rapid completion of the occupation.

The personnel of all echelons of the Corps conducted themselves in keeping with the highest traditions of the Military and Naval Service. It was a high privilege to command these troops.

The original caption to this image states: 'Iwo Jima, February 21, 1945. Agony on Iwo: Marines carefully slide a poncho under Corporal W. H. Porter, a victim of Japanese mortar fire on Iwo, preparatory to bearing him off for hospital care.' Corporal William Henry Porter was a member of the Headquarter Company, 1st Battalion, 26th Marines, 5th Marine Division. (USMC)

The original caption to this image states: 'Iwo Jima, February 20, 1945. Buddy to the Rescue: A wounded Marine gets a lift from a comrade after he was wounded by Japanese mortar fire on Iwo. Casualties were treated at front line aid stations and evacuated to rear bases for further medical attention.' (USMC)

Severe trauma wounds resulted from, gunshot, artillery, mortars, and rockets. Often these wounds resulted in extensive blood loss and severe shock. A lifesaving factor for many wounded men was the availability of whole blood. The landing force medical facilities alone used 5,406 pints, and the total used for the care of Iwo Jima patients up to D+25 reached 12,600, or slightly less than one pint per man evacuated. (USMC)

The original caption to this image states: 'Marines Returning with Wounded, Iwo Jima, 1945. EVERYWHERE MORTARS – Marine stretcher bearers bring back a Marine casualty while the Jap mortars, which played among the Leatherneck troops like rain, fire on the area. The men have taken advantage of a sunken path to gain a little protection on Iwo Jima.' The detail associated with this photos locates it at the northern end of the island. (USMC)

The original caption to this image states: 'Wounded Marines Returning to Aid Stations, Iwo Jima, 1945. THE ROAD BACK – Through the mortar fire of the enemy occasionally sweeps this road, the Marines wounded are sent back to the aid stations on Iwo Jima as quickly as humanly possible. These men have received first aid, the large tags are information on their wound and treatment, and they are walking back aiding each other on the journey.' (USMC)

The original caption to this image states: 'Marine Aid Station, Iwo Jima, 1945. AID STATION – Marines, wounded in the battle for Iwo Jima, are sheltered in a Japanese concrete air raid shelter which was not completely destroyed in the three-day bombardment and aerial attack preceding the landing. The Americans are in the unharmed portions of the thirty-foot shelter which received a hit in the middle.' (USMC)

As I reached in my surgical bag for a rat-toothed forceps and a curved-bladed scissors, I said, 'Get a handful of surgical sponges and roll him on over on his back.' When the man lay on his back, thrashing about as he struggled to try to overcome his airway obstruction, I was at last able to locate a large fragment of jaw bone wedged in the back of his throat. The bone fragment was readily grasped by the rat-toothed forceps and removed, while the soft tissue to which it was still attached was snipped through. The patient gratefully took several unimpeded lungfuls of air. His shattered facial structures presented a grotesque appearance and I wondered how our plastic surgeons would ever restore this man's identity.

The other casualty was also soon ready for transport, even though his pupils were dilated and his condition comatose. Rhoe had deftly covered the head and shoulder wounds with sterile dressings. Maloney had started a unit of plasma, which was entering the man's veins at sixty drops a minute. I sent Rhoe out to round up some transportation and Maloney to search the wounded man's backpack for warm clothes. He was still in deep shock … Rhoe returned with an empty weasel that had just deposited a load of ammunition farther to the west. Our two wounded men were quickly placed aboard. The assistant driver was instructed in the proper handling of the plasma bottle, so the lifegiving fluid would continue to run until he was received aboard one of our hospital ships.

*Lieutenant (MC) James S. Vedder, United States Navy, 3rd Battalion*
*Medical Officer, 27th Marines, 5th Marine Division*

The original caption to this image states: 'Marine Aid Station on Beach, Iwo Jima, 1945. PLASMA WARD – Navy doctors and corpsmen administer to wounded Marines at an aid station established in a gully on Iwo Jima. The high casualty rate in this operation required the use of gallons of plasma and whole blood sent by air from the West Coast.' (USMC)

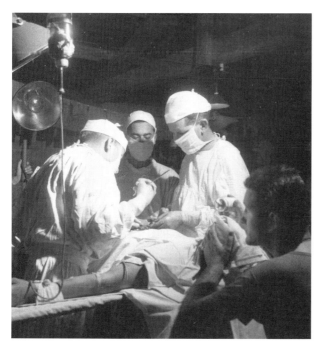

The original caption to this image states: 'Surgery in Fourth Marine Division Evacuation Hospital, Iwo Jima, 1945. MAYO CLINIC-IWO VERSION – While a Corpsman administers the other, Navy doctors operate to remove shrapnel from the abdomen of a wounded Leatherneck. The scene is the Fourth Marine Division evacuation hospital, functioning at an abandoned Japanese dugout several thousand yards from the front lines on Iwo Jima.' (USMC)

The USS *Bountiful* (AH-9), one of the hospital ships operating at Iwo Jima. Originally constructed as a US Navy transport, USS *Henderson* (AP-1) on 17 June 1916, the ship was converted to a hospital ship and renamed *Bountiful* in 1943. The ship departed San Francisco on 1 April 1944 for the Pacific and supported the operations during the invasion of the Marianas. *Bountiful* remained at Manus until 17 September, then sailed for the Palaus to bring casualties of the Peleliu landing to hospitals in the Solomon Islands. From there *Bountiful* operated between Leyte and the rear bases carrying veterans of the Philippines campaign. She departed Manus on 24 February for Ulithi and Saipan to receive casualties of the Iwo Jima assault. Following the assault on Iwo Jima she served at Okinawa and provided support for the occupation forces on mainland Japan. After the war the ship supported the atomic bomb testing at Bikini Atoll. Decommissioned, *Bountiful* was sold for scrap by the Maritime Commission on 28 January 1948, to Consolidated Builders Inc., Seattle.

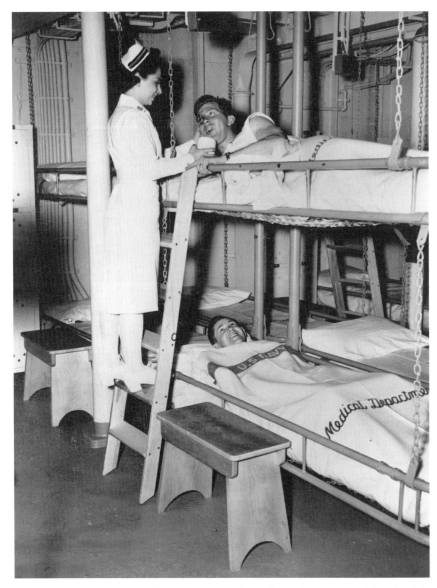

The original caption to this image states: 'Aboard the Navy Hospital Ship – USS Bountiful (AH-9). A US Navy nurse cares for two injured servicemen.' (USN)

At the same time we were boarding the troop ship, the Navy crewmen were using hoists to lift the wounded on board. The wounded were brought along the side of the ship by higgin boats and from the looks of the number of wounded coming in; we were going to be here for a while. Several of the Corpsmen remained in their higgin boats in order to continue tending to the wounded. As soon as they pulled up alongside and the wounded were hoisted upon deck, the Corpsmen on deck took over. It was a great sight to see, the way the Corpsmen were taking care of our wounded Marines.

*Sergeant John Ryland Thurman, 27th Regiment,*
*5th Marine Division*

On D+13, evacuation by air was initiated and requests for planes were made daily, with 2,449 patients airlifted to the Marianas. The wounded were examined by flight surgeons before take-off to make sure they could survive air travel, and corpsmen or naval nurses accompanied each flight. (USMC)

The 4th Marine Division cemetery on Iwo Jima. A total of 6,326 men were recorded as having died in action or died of wounds during the action to take the island. Three cemeteries were set up on the island, one for each Marine division. Corps troops, corps artillery and garrison troops were buried within the 5th Marine Division cemetery as the establishment of a separate cemetery was considered infeasible due to limited space on the island. Those that died aboard ships were buried at sea in water of a depth of over 100 fathoms. The number of dead recorded buried at sea is as eight officers and 136 enlisted men. In 1968, jurisdiction of the island was returned to Japan. The cemeteries were closed and the fallen were reburied, principally in Hawaii or their hometowns. (USN)

Servicemen gather to pay their respects at the 4th Marine Division cemetery on Iwo Jima on 15 March. (USMC)

A Marine bugler plays the last post during a dedication ceremony at a Marine cemetery on Iwo Jima. (USMC)

Marines seek out the graves of dead comrades after dedication of the 4th Marine Division cemetery. These cemeteries were laid out by the graves registration units, which was unpleasant and difficult work carried out largely unrecognized. They enabled a decent and respectful burial and a chance for colleagues and friends to pay respects, as these men are doing. Without the important work carried out by grave registration units, cemeteries such as these would not have existed. (USN)

The 4th Marine Division cemetery was located just inland from Blue 2 beach, seen from the air.

Behind every casualty figure or grave marker is a human being. Private Lee Sherman Bosworth served with Company E, 2nd Battalion, 26th Marines, 5th Marine Division, and was killed in action on 14 March. Shown is his grave marker on Iwo Jima as well as his photograph. He was nineteen when he was killed. (USN)

Private Lee Bosworth (on the left) had sent a happy birthday V-mail (reproduced below) to his mother, Bernice, before he left the USA. It read:

Dear Mom;
Hi mom! Happy birthday and all that stuff. How are you mom? Ok I bet.

Sorry I couldn't get you a regular card but it just isn't possible where I'm at so I made one out of this v-mail and I hope it gets to you in time. I'm going to send some money home and you can use it for Christmas presents if you want to cause I don't need it here.

Haven't been doing a darn thing to amount to anything except work. I've had one hour of sleep in 3 days and 2 nights but they let us sleep in this morning so I don't feel so bad now. Just all wore out in general I guess. Oh yes you take this money and get yourself something too remember now.

Well mom I had better close now and write tomorrow if I get the chance. So all my love to the swellest mom of all the world on her 38th birthday many happy more of them.

All My Love, Lee

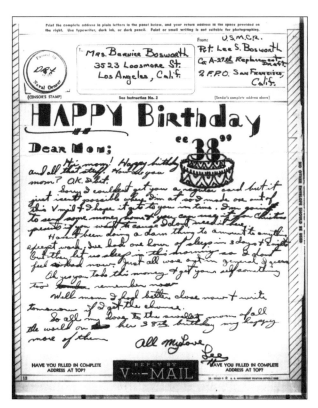

Lee is buried in the Glen Haven Memorial Park, Sylmar, Los Angeles County, California. Lest We Forget.

# Congressional Medal of Honor Citations

Pharmacist's Mate First Class Francis Pierce, U.S. Navy, serving with 2nd Battalion, 24th Marines, 4th Marine Division was awarded the Congressional Medal of Honor. The citation states:

For conspicuous gallantry and intrepidity at the risk of his life above and beyond the call of duty while attached to the 2nd Battalion, 24th Marines, 4th Marine Division, during the Iwo Jima campaign, 15 and 16 March 1945. Almost continuously under fire while carrying out the most dangerous volunteer assignments, Pierce gained valuable knowledge of the terrain and disposition of troops. Caught in heavy enemy rifle and machinegun fire which wounded a corpsman and 2 of the 8 stretcher bearers who were carrying 2 wounded Marines to a forward aid station on 15 March, Pierce quickly took charge of the party, carried the newly wounded men to a sheltered position, and rendered first aid. After directing the evacuation of 3 of the casualties, he stood in the open to draw the enemy's fire and, with his weapon blasting, enabled the litter bearers to reach cover. Turning his attention to the other 2 casualties he was attempting to stop the profuse bleeding of 1 man when a Japanese fired from a cave less than 20 yards away and wounded his patient again. Risking his own life to save his patient, Pierce deliberately exposed himself to draw the attacker from the cave and destroyed him with the last of his ammunition. Then lifting the wounded man to his back, he advanced unarmed through deadly rifle fire across 200 feet of open terrain. Despite exhaustion and in the face of warnings against such a suicidal mission, he again traversed the same fire-swept path to rescue the remaining marine. On the following morning, he led a combat patrol to the sniper nest and, while aiding a stricken Marine, was seriously wounded. Refusing aid for himself, he directed treatment for the casualty, at the same time maintaining protective fire for his comrades. Completely fearless, completely devoted to the care of his patients, Pierce inspired the entire battalion. His valor in the face of extreme peril sustains and enhances the finest traditions of the U.S. Naval Service.

Pharmacist's Mate Third Class Jack Williams, U.S. Navy, serving with 3rd Battalion, 28th Marines, 5th Marine Division:

For conspicuous gallantry and intrepidity at the risk of his life above and beyond the call of duty while serving with the 3rd Battalion 28th Marines, 5th Marine Division, during the occupation of Iwo Jima Volcano Islands, March 3, 1945. Gallantly going forward on the frontlines under intense enemy small-arms fire to assist a marine wounded in a fierce grenade battle, Williams dragged the man to a shallow depression and was kneeling, using his own body as a screen from the sustained fire as he administered first aid, when struck in the abdomen and groin 3 times by hostile rifle fire. Momentarily stunned, he quickly recovered and completed his ministration before applying battle dressings to his own multiple wounds. Unmindful of his own urgent need for medical attention, he remained in the perilous fire-swept area to care for another marine casualty. Heroically completing his task despite pain and profuse bleeding, he then endeavoured to make his way to the rear in search of adequate aid for himself when struck down by a Japanese sniper bullet which caused his collapse. Succumbing later as a result of his self-sacrificing service to others, Williams, by his courageous determination, unwavering fortitude and valiant performance of duty, served as an inspiring example of heroism, in keeping with the highest traditions of the U.S. Naval Service. He gallantly gave his life for his country.

Pharmacist's Mate Second Class George Edward Wahlen, U.S. Navy, serving with 2nd Battalion, 26th Marines, 5th Marine Division:

For conspicuous gallantry and intrepidity at the risk of his life above and beyond the call of duty while serving with the 2nd Battalion, 26th Marines, 5th Marine Division, during action against enemy Japanese forces on Iwo Jima in the Volcano group on 3 March 1945. Painfully wounded in the bitter action on 26 February, Wahlen remained on the battlefield, advancing well forward of the frontlines to aid a wounded marine and carrying him back to safety despite a terrific concentration of fire. Tireless in his ministrations, he consistently disregarded all danger to attend his fighting comrades as they fell under the devastating rain of shrapnel and bullets, and rendered prompt assistance to various elements of his combat group as required. When an adjacent platoon suffered heavy casualties, he defied the continuous pounding of heavy mortars and deadly fire of enemy rifles to care for the wounded, working rapidly in an area swept by constant fire and treating 14 casualties before returning to his own platoon. Wounded again on 2 March, he gallantly refused evacuation, moving out with his company the following day in a furious assault across 600 yards of open terrain and repeatedly rendering medical aid while exposed to the blasting fury of powerful Japanese guns. Stout-hearted and indomitable, he persevered in his determined efforts as his unit waged fierce battle and, unable to walk after sustaining a third agonizing wound, resolutely crawled 50 yards to administer first aid to still another fallen fighter. By his dauntless fortitude and valour, Wahlen served as a constant inspiration and contributed vitally to the high morale of his company during critical phases of this strategically important engagement. His heroic spirit of self-sacrifice in the face of overwhelming enemy fire upheld the highest traditions of the U.S. Naval Service.

# Chapter Ten

# Faces of Iwo Jima

This chapter aims to show images of the men who fought the battle of Iwo Jima to its victorious conclusion. The generation that fought a war against evil oppression were remarkable. Now aided by modern technology, it is still mostly young men who fight wars. Many years after conflicts have taken place, veterans, often very old, can provide a living link. It is important to remember these elderly veterans were once young and often at their prime when they fought; so many never came back. All in some way carried the experiences they had for the rest of their lives. In so many ways, the images speak for themselves.

The original caption to this image states: 'STEAM HEAT — Amid the vapors of the steam heat and sulphur pits in the background, Marines, (left to right) PFC David H. Christopher, of Nesquehoning, Pa., and Corporal Charles F. Parker, of Enid, Oklahoma, radioman and flame thrower, work on their equipment in their foxhole on Iwo Jima.' (USMC)

The original caption to this image states: 'GOING INLAND – Determination written on their countenances, Marines start the drive to the interior of Iwo Jima. Running at a crouch, they dart across the tableland in the shadow of Mount Suribachi, taking advantage of the scant protection offered by small rises in the volcanic sand.' The Marine in the foreground is armed with an M1 carbine, while his colleague standing behind him is carrying a 12 gauge riot-type pump-action shotgun. (USMC)

The original caption to this image states: 'Iwo Jima, February 20, 1945. West Coast Advance: While advancing up the west coast of the island, Marine Lieutenant R.A. Tilgham, gathered his men for briefing on the battlefield though they were under fire.' (USMC)

The original caption to this image states: 'DIVISION COMMAND POST – Officers of the 5th Marine Division direct the operation of their unit from a sandbagged position on Iwo Jima. They are, (left to right in the foreground): Brigadier General Leo D. Hermle, Assistant Division Commander; Major General Keller E. Rockey, (with phone), Division Commander; Colonel James F. Shaw, operations officer, and Colonel Ray Robinson, Division Chief of Staff.' (USMC)

The original caption to this image states: 'Marines Resting in Captured Japanese Machine Gun Emplacement, Iwo Jima, 1945. THEY CAN SMILE – In the shelter of the Japanese coastal gun emplacement on Iwo Jima, Marines undergoing the suffering of the severe fighting are able to smile as they rest for a few minutes. Note the shattered barrel of the cannon and the 60mm mortar in the foreground.' Examining the faces of these men, a range of emotions can be seen. (USMC)

A classic posed study of a Marine on Iwo Jima. He is armed with an M1 carbine and to his right is a partially repacked parachute. (USMC)

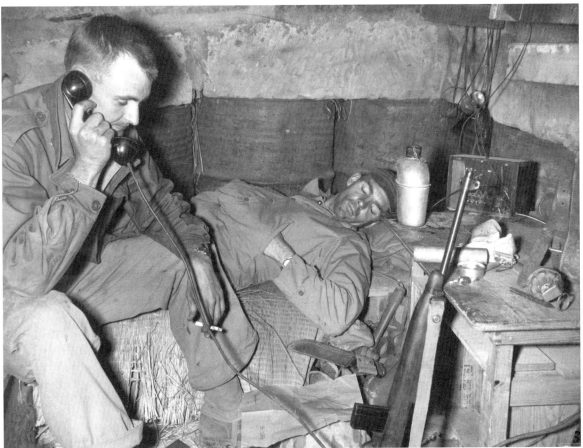

The original caption to this image states: 'OBSERVATION POST – This captured Japanese observation post is put to good use by two members of the Fifth Marine Division that stormed this Jap Pacific fortress of Iwo Jima. They are, (left to right): Captain Stanley C. McDaniel, of Duncan, Oklahoma, and Lieutenant Garfield M. Randall, Fairburg, Neb.' This bunker shows obvious Japanese construction, utilizing 50-gallon drums filled with sand or concrete. On the woodwork, Japanese markings can be seen. Captain McDaniel and Lieutenant Randall are surrounded by their equipment, which includes an M2 grenade on the table that has its fly-off lever taped down for safety. (USMC)

The commanding officer of the 3rd Marine Division, Major General Graves B. Erskine (centre), with two of his officers on Iwo Jima. A native of (Sikes, Winn Parish) Louisiana and a graduate of Louisiana State University, General Erskine had served with the Marines since 1917. He was a veteran of the First World War, during which he had been wounded and been awarded the Silver Star for bravery. Between the wars he had served in Santa Domingo, Puerto Rico, Nicaragua, and the American Embassy at Peking. When the Second World War broke out he was chief of staff of the Amphibious Force, Atlantic Fleet. (USMC)

The original caption to this image states: 'WELL DONE, THIRD – Following the formal flag raising on Iwo Jima, March 14, 1945, which officially announced a victory for the Marine and Naval forces seizing this Japanese possession in the Volcano Island group, Lieutenant General Holland M. Smith, (right) Commanding General of the Expeditionary Troops in the Iwo Jima Operation, congratulates Major General Graves B. Erskine, of La Jolla, California, Commanding General of the Third Marine Division, upon the splendid showing of the Third Division in the campaign.' (USMC)

Lieutenant General Holland M. Smith was an acknowledged American expert on amphibious operations. His fierce temper earned him the nickname 'Howling Mad'. Born in Hatchechubbee, Alabama, in 1882, he joined the Marine Corps in 1906 and served in the Dominican Republic. During the First World War, Smith served in France as a staff officer and as communications officer for 4 Regiment during the Belleau Wood campaign, where he was awarded the Croix de Guerre. Between the wars he studied amphibious doctrine. He was given command of 1 Marine Brigade in 1940 and promoted to major general in February 1941. At the outbreak of the war he was commander of the Fleet Marine Force and was transferred to the West Coast to organize the Pacific Fleet Amphibious Force in September 1942. On 5 September 1943, he took command of the V Amphibious Corps.

The original caption to this image states: 'IWO'S POST OFFICE TAKES SHAPE – A scant ten days after D-Day on Iwo Jima the mailmen came in. Here two members of the Fourth Marine Division post office get things "squared away." Painting the sign is Sergeant B.D. Bryant, of Spartansburg, Pa., while Corporal Kenneth E. Hales, of Pasco, Wasn., looks on.' (USMC)

The original caption to this image states: 'Corporal Edward Burckhardt, of Yonkers, New York, sports a kitten that he found at the base of Suribachi Yama on the battlefield at Iwo Jima when he came ashore with the 5th Marine Division.' Animals often feature with soldiers, perhaps reminding them of home. Even among the desolation of Iwo Jima this little cat has found somebody to look after it! (USMC)

Private Francis M. Hall with his Dobermann Pinscher on Iwo Jima in March 1945. The war dog platoons provided vital services on Iwo Jima as they were employed to indicate the presence of a hidden enemy, particularly ambushes, as well as providing night security. During clearance operation on Iwo Jima, the dogs were also used to indicate the presence of Japanese hiding in caves and other fortifications. (USMC)

The original caption to this image states: 'Photographed by D.G. Christian, February 24, 1945. This image is symbolic of the battle to capture Iwo Jima. A tough, injured but defiant – victorious Marine pictured in front of a wrecked Japanese Nakajima J1N1-S Gekko "IRVING" reconnaissance aircraft. Defeated Japanese aviation soon to make way for soon to be victorious American airpower.' (USMC)

# Chapter Eleven

# The Japanese

The exact number of Japanese defenders of on Iwo Jima when the island was attacked on 19 February is not known. The after-action report produced by V Amphibious Corps estimated that 13,449 of the defenders had been buried by the Japanese themselves with approximately 8,000 sealed in caves, a total of 21,449 dead. Over the period 19 February to 26 March, the V Amphibious Corps recorded capturing 112 Japanese and 159 Koreans – a total of 217 prisoners of war. The willingness of the Japanese soldier to fight to the end and not surrender is well documented. This can partly be explained by the Japanese armed forces being conditioned to this belief from the start of their military experiences, which was based on a brutalizing training regime. Often proven to be a heartless and barbaric enemy, the courage shown by many of the Japanese soldiers who died on Iwo Jima, however, cannot be doubted.

The Japanese tactics and defence of Iwo Jima were recognized as being sound and having succeeded in inflicting the maximum number of casualties to the attacking forces. The Japanese had determined that the deployment of large numbers of infantry on the landing beaches would not check a landing effectively under cover of intense naval and air bombardment. Therefore, the landing beaches were lightly held with infantry, a reliance being placed on delivering a heavy volume of artillery, rocket, mortar and anti-boat gunfire in an effort to make the beaches untenable. The attacking forces, however, succeeded in forcing a beachhead. After this, the Japanese fought a stubborn, well-planned defence from positions consisting of mutually supporting pillboxes, caves, covered emplacements and dug-in tanks, giving ground only when these defences were actually overrun. The tactics employed, coupled with the excellently prepared fortified positions and the rocky terrain, were the tactics that made the capture of Iwo Jima so long, difficult, and costly.

The Japanese were recognized as having conducted an intelligent, passive defence from successive highly organized positions. Many Japanese chose to end their own lives rather than surrender. Sergeant John Ryland Thurman of the 27th Marines related what he saw looking into a Japanese bunker:

I took a slow look inside. What I saw was weird and spooky. There were five Japanese Soldiers lying on their backs along the wall with the end of their rifle barrel stuck up under their chins. They had their big toe stuck in the trigger, using the toe to fire the rifle off the bullet going up thru the head. The impact from the bullet took nearly the whole tip of their head off scattering their skull bones and brains all over the bodies behind them. There was blood still running from their mouths and from under their chins. From the way it looked all five fired at the same time. They must have decided to commit suicide rather than being captured.

Dealing with the large numbers of enemy dead imposed a huge problem in relation to disposing of them. Enemy dead were sprayed with pesticides (DDT or sodium arsenite) to kill adult flies and keep them off the corpses. They were then buried as expeditiously as possible. It was not militarily feasible or practicable to centralize the collection and burial of enemy dead.

Actual burials of enemy dead by the landing force were as follows, to 18.00, 24 March:

| Corps Troops | 9 |
|---|---|
| Garrison Forces | 337 |
| 3rd Marine Division | 2,087 |
| 4th Marine Division | 3,296 |
| 5th Marine Division | 7,710 |
| Total | 13,449 |

The original caption to this image states: 'ANY REMAINING? – Beside the body of a slain Japanese officer, Marine Corporal Marling Hoge, cautiously watched the terrain ahead for any Jap snipers or stragglers, on Iwo Jima. During the initial phases of the attack, few dead Japanese were in evidence. Whilst an organised defence took place they were collected by their colleagues. As the campaign wore on, then the Japanese became less able to collect their own dead and the finding of Japanese bodies became commonplace.' (USMC)

This image shows one of the big coastal guns emplaced on the island, part of the excellently prepared fortified positions.

The original caption to this image states: 'STILL THERE – Even after the preparatory naval bombardment reduced this reinforced concrete pillbox of the Japs to rubble, when the Marines landed on Iwo Jima they had to finish the crew at close range in the fighting on D-Day.' (USMC)

The original caption to this image states: 'Marines Explore Japanese Emplacement, Iwo Jima, 1945. SEEKERS – Wary Marines of the Fifth Division, search a demolished Jap pillbox on Iwo Jima in the first day's fighting, looking for lurking Japs who might open fire on the Marines' flanks.' (USMC)

The Japanese deployed a number of tanks in defence of the Island. This tank is a Type 95, armed with a 37mm gun. This image shows how difficult the terrain on the island became further inland and how this benefited the defenders.

The Type 95 tank shown from the rear. It has been well camouflaged and defensively dug-in. Difficult to attack from the front without superior firepower, a flanking attack would have been required.

This well dug-in Type 95 tank entrenched on the western slope of hill 382 shows the clear field of fire it possessed over airfield No. 2 and demonstrates the great skill with which the Japanese defenders located their defences.

One of the key features that enabled the Japanese to defend the island so tenaciously and prolong their defence was the use of underground tunnels and bunkers. Their soldiers had a considerable time to fortify the island by utilizing dug-in and subterranean defences. These proved extremely difficult and time-consuming to destroy.

Caves were destroyed one at a time, following a kind of 'blueprint' that we worked out over time. The riflemen in our squad, along with B.A.R. (Browning Automatic Rifle) men borrowed from the infantry unit we were supporting, would fire into the cave to keep any people inside from firing out. In the meantime Frank and I would work our way toward the cave, one on each side of the entrance. (He threw better left-handed, so he always took the right side, and I threw better right-handed, so I always took the left.). Before starting, we removed our cartridge belts and anything else that would make noise or hinder us as we crawled. We wore cloth utility caps instead of helmets. We carried a couple of grenades in the side pockets of our engineer pants and tucked .45 pistols under our belts at the small of our backs. This left us free to crawl, dragging our explosives. We would start forward, hopefully out of sight of anyone in the cave or bunker. In the case of caves, once we were in place and the moment was right, each of us would sling one of those 30-pound satchels of composition C into the opening. The two near-simultaneous explosions usually collapsed the roof in on those inside. These charges had thirty-second delay fuses, so in order to deprive cave occupants of a chance to throw them back out before they went off, we had to ignite the fuse and count a while before we threw them in. Even so, the occupants sometimes managed to throw one back. By throwing in two charges at nearly the same time we caused enough confusion inside that we never got both thrown back at us … After a cave was blown shut, often it would be silent only for a few hours. Then Japs would enter it from the tunnel complex that connected so many of the caves, poke a little hole through the dirt and rubble covering the entrance, and start firing at the Marines again. Some caves had to be 're-sealed' several times.

*Private First Class Howard N. McLaughlin Jr, USMCR, 5th Marine Division*

This image shows the entrance to a large tunnel system and demonstrates the sophistication of the Japanese tunnelling efforts. The defenders of these caves held on stubbornly, requiring a number of different measures to combat them. These included bulldozing the entrances to seal in those inside. Other measures included pumping sea water or fuel (or both) into them and setting fire to the fuel. The entrance to this tunnel led to a system that was 800 yards long and had fourteen entrances. It housed two battalion command posts.

We backed up weasel weapons carriers with a couple of 55-gallon drums full of diesel fuel and poured them into the cave. Well, then we set fire with a phosphorus grenade. And that was the end of that.

*Corporal Edward Mervich, 147th Infantry Regiment*

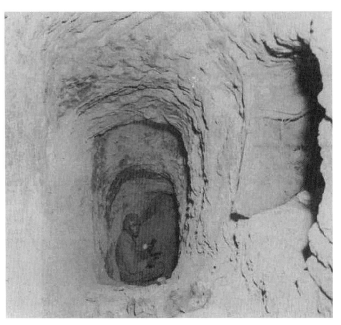

The inside of one of the tunnel systems. A Marine can be seen cautiously crouching inside.

Another view of the inside of one of the tunnel systems. The Marine is holding his .24 pistol ready and has a flashlight in his other hand.

War dogs were used to detect Japanese hiding in tunnels. They became highly effective at indicating the presence of enemy troops underground.

The Japanese defenders' view of a dog team from inside a tunnel. Not all such encounters ended with the death of the Japanese. Navy radioman Tsuruji Akikusa, coming to his senses in a U.S. Army field hospital, had explained to him by a fellow Japanese prisoner how he got there. He had been found unconscious by a dog team. Relating to the incident many years later, he stated: 'I owe my life to that American soldier and his dog who rescued me.'

Very few prisoners of war were taken but these men are surrendering. All prisoners of war were evacuated to ships designated for further evacuation to the Mariana Islands, with the exception of one officer and one enlisted man who were evacuated via air to the Joint Intelligence Centre, Pacific Ocean Areas, due to their military value necessitating immediate and detailed interrogation.

More Japanese surrendering. Two prisoners were retained by the 3rd Marine Division and one by the 5th Division to help efforts to get their colleagues to surrender. (USMC)

One of the prisoners taken on Iwo Jima is taken to the beach by 3rd Division Marines. This picture is dated 2 March 1945. (USN)

Many of the Japanese defenders met a traumatic end. Blasted by small arms fire, mortars, artillery and flame-throwers, their gruesome remains were quickly disposed of as soon as possible. Whenever possible the Japanese disposed of his own dead. The loose sandy soil favoured rapid burial, and the terrain and natural camouflage enabled movement of enemy burial parties at night. Where the situation would not permit removal of the dead, the Japanese often burned or buried them in pillboxes.

The last organized Japanese attack took place on the night of 25–26 March. This resulted in the deaths of most of the attackers, with casualties also being sustained by the American forces. The task of garrisoning the island was assigned to the U.S. Army 147th Infantry Regiment, which carried out the still difficult and dangerous mopping up operations.

The early part of the night of 25–26 March was relatively quiet. In the 3rd Mar Div. zone, RCT 9 killed 14 Japanese and captured 1 POW. The 147th Infantry: killed 7 Japanese in their area.

About 0515 a force of from 200 to 300 Japanese moving; down from the north attacked our troops located in TAs 198 and 215. The units engaged were the 5th Pioneer Bn, the 21st Fighter Group, the 465th Aviation Squadron, the 506th AAA Gun Bn, and the 98th NC Bn. The focal point of the counterattack was the area occupied by the 5th Pioneer Bn in TA 198S and on that unit developed the main burden of repelling it. The attack was carried out from three directions in echelon. The first two from the Southwest and South at about 0515, and the third from the North at 0715. The chief difficulty experienced by our forces was in distinguishing between hostile and friendly units. However, by 0830 the enemy, in this area had been annihilated and infantry units from 5th Mar Div and the 167th Infantry assumed the task of patrolling and completing mopping up in the surrounding areas. The total of enemy dead was 223, 196 of those being found in the areas in which the 5th Pioneer Bn engaged the enemy. It should be noted that this attack was not a banzai charge but was carefully calculated to achieve the maximum confusion and destruction before its inevitable annihilation. Our casualties were not heavy however, the heaviest being in the aviation elements involved.

The 5th Pioneer Bn reported that 196 enemy killed in their area were armed with Japanese rifles and U. S. carbines and BARS. About 40 carried swords indicating a high percentage of officers and senior NCOs. Rations appeared ample being a mixture of U.S. rations. No shortage of water was apparent. Many of the Japanese showed evidence of previous wounds. A POW taken by 3rdMArDIV stated that Lt Gen KURIBAYASHI and other senior officers were in this attack force but examination of bodies, captured swords and documents failed to confirm this assertion.

*5th Amphibious Corps, Report on Operations for the*
*Invasion and Capture of Iwo Jima*

First Lieutenant Harry Linn Martin, USMCR, Company C, 5th Pioneer Battalion, 5th Marine Division was awarded the Congressional Medal of Honor. His citation states:

For conspicuous gallantry and intrepidity at the risk of his life above and beyond the call of duty as platoon leader attached to Company C, 5th Pioneer Battalion, 5th Marine Division, in action against enemy Japanese forces on Iwo Jima, Volcano Islands, 26 March 1945. With his sector of the 5th Pioneer Battalion bivouac area penetrated by a concentrated enemy attack launched a few minutes before dawn, 1st Lieutenant Martin instantly organized a firing line with the Marines nearest his foxhole and succeeded in checking momentarily the headlong rush of the Japanese. Determined to rescue several of his men trapped in positions overrun by the enemy, he defied intense hostile fire to work his way through the Japanese to the surrounded Marines. Although sustaining 2 severe wounds, he blasted the Japanese who attempted to intercept him, located his beleaguered men and directed them to their own lines. When 4 of the infiltrating enemy took possession of an abandoned machinegun pit and subjected his sector to a barrage of hand grenades, 1st Lieutenant Martin, alone and armed only with a pistol, boldly charged the hostile position and killed all of its occupants. Realizing that his few remaining comrades could not repulse another organized attack, he called to his men to follow and then charged into the midst of the strong enemy force, firing his weapon and scattering them until he fell, mortally wounded by a grenade. By his outstanding valor, indomitable fighting spirit and tenacious determination in the face of overwhelming odds, 1st Lieutenant Martin permanently disrupted a coordinated Japanese attack and prevented a greater loss of life in his own and adjacent platoons. His inspiring leadership and unswerving devotion to duty reflect the highest credit upon himself and the U.S. Naval Service. He gallantly gave his life in the service of his country.

First Lieutenant Martin is buried in Oakwood Cemetery, Bucyrus, Crawford County, Ohio.

Photographed by Technical Sergeant Kress, this epitaph was created by Marines for five dead Japanese. Carved into a piece of rock, it reads 'Hirno Iwo, Sino Iwo, Spikno Iwo and NoMo Iwo' ('Hear no Iwo, See no Iwo, Speak no Iwo, No more Iwo'). (USN)

# Chapter Twelve

# Strike Base and Safe Haven

The primary objective in relation to capturing Iwo Jima was to support air operations against the Japanese mainland. As soon as practically possible, work had begun to make the airstrips on the island operational. Elements of the Army's 386th Air Service Group had come ashore on 3 March and the first aircraft to land on the island were Marine observation Stinson OY-1 Sentinel aircraft, which landed on 26 February. The first large aircraft to arrive was a US Navy Douglas R4D hospital plane nicknamed *Peg O'My Heart*, followed by a Marine Curtiss R5C carrying 81mm mortar ammunition. The first of B-29 bombers to land on the island arrived the next day, 4 March, when an aircraft of the 9th Bomb Group operating from Saipan that had attacked the Nakajima Musashino aircraft plant near Tokyo made an emergency landing.

Mustangs of the 47th Fighter Squadron, belonging to the 15th Fighter Group, flew to the island on 6 March from Saipan. The three squadrons (45th, 47th and 78th Fighter Squadrons) of the 15th Fighter Group, along with aircraft of the 21st Fighter Group (which arrived on 21 March) initially flew missions supporting the troops on Iwo Jima and also attacked the Japanese-held island of Chichi Jima (approximately 168 miles to the north-east). The first very long-range mission took place on 7 April, in which nearly 100 Mustangs took off to support 103 B-29 bombers of the 73rd Bomb Wing.

The successful capture of the island now meant that aircraft in trouble could land there. Fighter escorts flew from Iwo Jima, bomber formations assembled over the island and could refuel there. If aircraft had to ditch or crews had to bail out then air-sea rescue units from Iwo Jima could pick them up. The island became a vital life-saver for the B-29 bomber crews. Along with fighter aircraft flying escort missions, search and rescue aircraft, anti-submarine and anti-shipping strike aircraft also flew from Iwo Jima. P-61 night fighter aircraft were also based on the island and flew protective combat air patrols, intruder, anti-shipping, search and rescue and weather missions.

Iwo Jima also played a part in the dropping of the two atomic bombs on Japan. Prior to this, the commander and crew of the aircraft that would drop the first bomb on 6 August, Colonel Paul Tibbets, visited Iwo Jima. A specially reinforced concrete pit had been built on the island to be used in the event that *Enola Gay*, Tibbets' aircraft, developed a mechanical fault en route to Japan. The pit would be used to transfer the bomb to a reserve aircraft standing by for this purpose. Ultimately, of course, the pit was not required. The crew of *Enola Gay* visited Iwo Jima on the way to drop their bomb on Hiroshima, this time the purpose being to rendezvous with support aircraft. Arriving at 05.52, *Enola Gay* circled the island at 9,300ft before heading off on the mission.

The island nearly became host to *Bockscar*, the B-29 that dropped the second atomic bomb on Nagasaki on 9 August. *Bockscar* had developed a fuel transfer problem but the crew had elected to fly the aircraft and planned to land on Iwo Jima. However, due to difficulties locating the primary target (Kokura) and having to divert to the secondary target, Nagasaki, the aircraft had used up too much fuel to reach Iwo Jima and was forced to land on Okinawa.

Iwo Jima became not only a strike base, taking the war to Japan, but also a safe haven for countless US airmen whose aircraft were short on fuel, had critically wounded men on board or had sustained damage and needed to land as soon as possible.

Mustangs of the 15th Fighter Group lined up on the island. The Mustangs providing fighter escort to bombers attacking the Japanese mainland were required to fly very long distances. The return trip from Iwo Jima to Tokyo took more than seven hours and was 622 miles, all of it over the Pacific Ocean. Mount Suribachi can be seen in the background.

B-29 *Dinah Might* shortly after landing on Iwo Jima on 6 March. This aircraft was the first to use the island for an emergency landing. *Dinah Might* had experienced a problem when its bomb bay doors failed to close. The drag caused by this failure meant the aircraft would not have sufficient fuel to return to its base at Tinian. Iwo Jima at this time was not formally available as an emergency landing ground due to the battle still raging there.

The pilot, Lieutenant Fred Malo, however, elected to land as the B-29 developed a further problem with the fuel system, giving little other option other than ditching the aircraft in the sea. Lieutenant Malo successfully landed the aircraft on the runway of No. 2 airfield, having made his approach from the south, flying past Mount Suribachi. The problems were fixed and the bomber later flew off to return to Tinian. The aircraft had been subjected to enemy fire both during landing and take-off. *Dinah Might* made a further stop on Iwo Jima more than a month later. All the crew with the exception of one of gunners, Sergeant Robert Brackett, who had been left behind in charge of the aircraft, were flown back to Tinian on another B-29. Sadly, they were later killed on a mission over Kawasaki, leaving Sergeant Brackett as the sole survivor of the crew. (USMC)

Relaxed is not quite the word for it. You suddenly realize that you are extremely fatigued, thirsty, and almost unable to fly the plane. The parachute harness irritates your neck, the sun is too hot, and worst of all you discover you are 'butt sprung.' There is no position in which you can get rid of the ache in your sitting apparatus for more than a minute or two. You let air out of your seat cushion, and it feels wonderful, then the ache returns. You let the air back in the cushion, and you're fine again for a minute. After a while, you exercise some God-given power to just ignore it. Now you pass Kita Jima, forty miles to go, and then Iwo. You revive yourself enough now to land and taxi your airplane in, wave to your crew chief and resolve to jump out of the plane to show what a hardy fellow you are, but after releasing the harness, you can't raise yourself. So, I sat there for a while filling out forms, telling the crew chief how we fared, and then tried again — no luck. About this time the flight surgeon's helper crawled up on the wing with a shot of mission whiskey. Ah, here's the thing for quick strength, so I took the two ounces and downed it like World War I pilots and cowboys were supposed to do. No luck, all I did was get sick. So, I graciously allowed Sergeant Pesci, my crew chief, to lift me out of the cockpit and help me to the ground. A little walking around and I revived enough to be self-mobile.

*Major Harry C. Crim, Squadron Commander, 72nd Squadron,*
*21st Fighter Group*

A P-51 Mustang powers up ready to take off from Iwo Jima.

B-29 *Miss Judy* of the 462nd Bomb Group making an emergency landing on Iwo Jima, one of many made by these large aircraft.

Boeing B-29s of the 21st Bomber Command lined up on Iwo Jima.

This B-29 crash-landed on Iwo Jima in mid-March. First on the scene would be the crash and medical teams. A crowd of onlookers would undoubtedly follow the progress of the landing hoping that it would make it down in one piece.

The propeller of this 505th Bomb Group aircraft sheared off and struck the main body of the aircraft. The errant propeller then bounced off the fuselage and struck the propeller blade of the remaining engine. It was able to make a safe landing on Iwo Jima.

Bad weather could prevent an aircraft landing on Iwo Jima. This aircraft had attempted to land on 26 March but was prevented from doing so as a result of the island being fog-bound. If unable to land, the options for the crew were to either ditch or bail out. The crew of this aircraft of the 6th Bomb Group chose the ditching option. An attempt to tow the aircraft to shore failed and it eventually disappeared into the ocean.

A Marine stands guard on an old Japanese anti-aircraft position overlooking the airfield. (USMC)

The victors and the vanquished. A flight of Mustangs taking off from Iwo Jima. In the foreground the wrecked remains of a Japanese Zero fighter can be seen.

# Chapter Thirteen

# Aftermath

As the amphibious assault combat phase ended, Marine and attached units were withdrawn from the island with a relief in place being carried out by the US Army's 147th Infantry Regiment. On 4 April, the 147th Infantry relieved the last Marine unit on the island (the 9th Marine Regiment) and from that point onward became solely responsible for the clearing actions on Iwo Jima as well as acting as its defence force. On the island, the remains of the Japanese defences and detritus lay scattered around. Mopping up operations continued until June, when the last of the Japanese defenders who had been hiding were cleared up.

The price had been high, but the island was worth it. From the airfields that had been won by the heroism and sacrifices of the men of the Third, Fourth and Fifth Marine Divisions. American fighter planes would soon be taking off for Tokyo. Crippled B-29s returning from Japan would have a friendly base on which to land.

*Lieutenant John C. Chapin, 'The Fifth Marine Division in World War II'*

The island was littered with destroyed Japanese equipment. Here, Marines examine a wrecked Japanese Betty bomber. Photographed by Don Fox on 26 February. (USN)

A Marine examines a knocked out Japanese Type 97 medium tank. (USN)

A battered and knocked out twin 25mm anti-aircraft position, one of many that had defended the Island. Marked around the edge of the walls are bearing markers – in English. (USMC)

Scores of wrecked Japanese planes littered the island, victims of pre-invasion strikes. These Marines are walking past a large pile of destroyed Japanese aircraft. On the right, the substantial remains of a Mitsubishi G3M Nell bomber can be seen. Photographed by Technical Sergeant George B. Kress on 23 February. (USN)

An abandoned Marine M4 Sherman tank stranded – bogged in – in the loose black sand that prevailed on and near the beaches. (USMC)

Captured Japanese ammunition and equipment, not only of interest to intelligence operatives but souvenir hunters as well. (USMC)

The original caption to this image states: 'WATER TANKS – On the sun-blistered island of Iwo Jima, the question of water was vital to both the Marines and the Japs. The enemy had prepared himself with the construction of these five storage tanks which now show evidence of shelling.' (USMC)

The Japanese defences utilized an array of weapons, including this crude 200mm rocket launcher. It had an approximate range of 5,000 yards and an explosive charge of 310lb. This is a captured example. (USN)

Marines departing the island on an LST. (USMC)

Iwo is now under new management! Published both in the English and Japanese language, this original Japanese sign warned that: 'Trespassing, surveying, photographing, sketching, modelling, etc., upon or of these premises, without previous official permission, are prohibited by the Military Secret Law. Any offender in this regard will be punished by [two words struck out] law.' (USMC)

I landed with the 28th Marines and had good friends among them Theirs had been the task of taking Suribachi at the first, the key to the operation, and they took it. Then, with a few days' rest, they were on the front lines almost steadily until the very end, and it fell to their lot to hit that deep gorge with its hive of caves, which the Japs chose for the final stand. And chose well. I was on the beach when the 28th came down to re-embark. They had finished the Gorge only the day before. They were cheerful, for they were getting off the island now, but they were quiet men. They would smile instead of laugh. You couldn't distinguish officers from men—all dusty, all weary, nearly all heavily bearded.

A battalion sergeant major stopped to pass a word with a sergeant I was talking to. The sergeant said he was looking forward to getting back into camp and coming over to the battalion's sergeants' mess for a good meal once again. A battalion's normal complement of sergeants is sixty-nine. "Well I got six now," he said, "six from sixty-nine."

*Sergeant Francis W. Cockrel, 28th Marines, 5th Marine Division*

Chaplain John H. Craven, Regimental Chaplain, 14th Marines, conducts services on the hatch of a troop transport returning from Iwo Jima in March 1945. (USMC)

In 1949, what would become an iconic film portraying the attack on Iwo Jima, *Sands of Iwo Jima*, was filmed, featuring John Wayne in the starring role. Here, Major General Graves B. Erskine talks with John Wayne during the filming. The film's director, Allan Dwann, is in the centre. (USMC)

On the set of *Sands of Iwo Jima*. From right to left, stars Forrest Tucker and John Wayne, Lieutenant General Holland M. Smith Retd., director Allan Dwan and Major General Graves B. Erskine. The flag used in the original flag-raising ceremony was used in the segment of the film representing the event. (USMC)

# Chapter Fourteen

# Iwo Jima Today

The island of Iwo Jima was formally handed back to the Japanese on 26 June 1968. Renamed Iōtō (Ioto), it is still retained as a Japanese military base. The vegetation blasted during the battle grew back many years ago and now covers most of the battle-scarred landscape. However, relics of war can still be seen, along with some of the island's fortifications. While the American cemeteries here were relocated, the remains of many of the Japanese defenders are still interred on the island in unmarked, unknown grave locations or entombed underground. After many years, Japan now actively works to recover its war dead from the island.

U.S. Marine Staff Sergeant Paul Walker, Headquarters Company, Marine Corps Security Force Regiment, holds up an unused American round found in the sand of the beach during a visit to the island in December 2014. (US Department of Defense)

**176** Not related to the actual battle itself, this image shows the remains of blockships sunk in 1945 to help form a sheltered unloading point. (US Department of Defense)

The memorial at the summit of Mount Suribachi is located where the original flag-raising ceremony took place. (US Department of Defense)

A rusting coastal gun. (US Department of Defense)

One of the many tunnel entrances that still exist on Iwo Jima. Tunnels such as this still contain the remains of the Japanese defenders. (US Department of Defense)

Some of the tunnels built by the Japanese are accessible today. (US Department of Defense)

Relics inside one of the tunnels. The object on the right inside the box is part of a Japanese respirator. (US Department of Defense)

Today, the United States Marine Corps War Memorial represents their country's gratitude to the Marines and those who have fought beside them. The memorial is based on the iconic Joe Rosenthal image of the raising of the flag on Mount Suribachi. The memorial was created by sculptor Felix W. de Weldon and was initially completed in plaster, before it was carefully disassembled and moved to Brooklyn, New York, for casting in bronze. The casting process took nearly three years. The nearly 78ft tall monument was made in approximately a dozen pieces, the largest weighing more than 20 tons. It was then taken to Arlington Ridge Park, Washington, D.C., and assembled. The memorial was dedicated by President Dwight D. Eisenhower in a ceremony on 10 November 1954. (USMC)

The Marine Corps Memorial. (Courtesy of Adrian R. Rowan)

Whilst the battle to take the island of Iwo Jima lives on in history, it also lives on in the memory of those who were there. To close this book, it is only fitting to leave the last comment on behalf of all of them to a veteran of the assault to take the island.

As a combat corpsman with the 1st Battalion, B Company, 9th Marine Regiment, I served thirty full days on the line with the gallant Marines … and gallant they were! Let it be known that every mother's son was a hero on that God-forsaken island, also known by those of us who fought there as 'Bloody Iwo.' *Semper Fi.*

*John A. 'Doc' Connolly, age 92, 11 May 2018*

# Appendix I

# List of Key Dates Relating to the Battle of Iwo Jima

21 February   The 21st Marines (VAC Reserve) committed in 4th Division zone of action.

23 February   American Flag raised atop Mount Suribachi by the 28th Marines.

25 February   The 3rd Marine Division (less 3rd Marines) committed in battle for Iwo. General unloading of cargo begins.

27 February   The 3rd Division overruns Airfield Number 2, Hills PETER and 199-OBOE.

2 March   Marines of the 5th Division overrun Hill 362A.

3 March   Marines of the 3rd Division clear Airfield Number 3. The 3rd Division makes predawn attack against Hill 362C. Hill captured later in the day.

8 March   Japanese night counter-attack (night of 8–9 March) repulsed by 4th Division.

10 March   4th Division troops break through to the east coast, pinch out enemy salient around Amphitheater and Turkey Knob.

11 March   Iwo-based Army Air Force fighter planes assume responsibility for providing air defence and ground support missions when last Navy escort carriers leave.

14 March   Official flag-raising ceremony marks proclamation of U.S. Navy Military Government in Volcano Islands. Commander, Expeditionary Troops, departs for Guam.
First Marine units commence loading out for departure from Iwo.

16 March   Last enemy opposition crushed in 3rd Division zone with elimination of Cushman's Pocket. Final Japanese resistance destroyed in 4th Division zone as last enemy held pocket is wiped out. Iwo Jima declared secured at 18.00 after twenty-six days of bitter fighting.

20 March   147th Infantry Regiment (USA) arrives for garrison duty.

# Appendix II

# V Amphibious Corps
# Order of Battle

<u>V Amphibious Corps, Major General Harry Schmidt</u>

<u>3rd Division, Major General Graves B. Erskine</u>
9th Regiment, Colonel Howard N. Kenyon
1st Battalion, Lieutenant Colonel Carey A. Randall/Major William T.
Glass/Lieutenant Colonel Jack F. Warner
2nd Battalion, Lieutenant Colonel Robert E. Chusman, Jr.
2nd Battalion, Lieutenant Colonel Harold C. Boehm

21st Regiment, Colonel Hartnoll J. Withers
1st Battalion, Lieutenant Colonel Marlowe C. Williams/Major Clay M. Murray/Major
   Robert H. Houser
2nd Battalion, Lieutenant Colonel Lowell E. English/Major George S. Percy
3rd Battalion, Lieutenant Colonel Wendell H. Duplantis

12th Regiment [Artillery], Lieutenant Colonel Raymond F. Crist, Jr.
1st Battalion, Major George B. Thomas
2nd Battalion, Lieutenant Colonel William T. Fairbourn
3rd Battalion, Lieutenant Colonel Alpha L. Bowser, Jr.
4th Battalion, Major Joe B. Wallen

3rd Tank Battalion, Major Holly H. Evans
3rd Engineer Battalion, Lieutenant Colonel Walter S. Campbell
3rd Pioneer Battalion, Lieutenant Colonel Edmund M. Williams
3rd Service Battalion, Lieutenant Colonel Paul G. Chandler
3rd Motor Transport Battalion, Lieutenant Colonel Ernest W. Fry, Jr.
3rd Medical Battalion, Commander Anthony E. Reymont, USNR
3rd Joint Assault Signal Company (JASCO)
Marine Observation Squadron 1
3rd War Dog Platoon
JICPOA Intelligence Team

4th Division, Major General Clifton B. Cates:
23rd Regiment, Colonel Walter W. Wensinger
1st Battalion, Lieutenant Colonel Ralph Haas/Lieutenant Colonel Louis B. Blissard
2nd Battalion, Major Robert H. Davidson/Lieutenant Colonel Edward J. Dillon
3rd Battalion, Major James F. Scales

24th Regiment, Colonel Walter I. Jordan
1st Battalion, Major Paul S. Treitel/Lieutenant Colonel Austin R. Brunelli
2nd Battalion, Lieutenant Colonel Richard Rothwell
3rd Battalion, Lieutenant Colonel Alexander A. Vandegrift, Jr./Major Doyle A. Stout

25th Regiment, Colonel John R. ('Pat') Lanigan
1st Battalion, Lieutenant Colonel Hollis U. Mustain/Major Fenton J. Mee
2nd Battalion, Lieutenant Colonel Lewis C. Hudson, Jr./Lieutenant Colonel James Taul
3rd Battalion, Lieutenant Colonel Justice M. Chambers/Captain James C. Headley

14th Regiment [Artillery], Colonel Louis G. De Haven
1st Battalion, Major John B. Edgar, Jr.
2nd Battalion, Major Clifford B. Drake
3rd Battalion, Lieutenant Colonel Robert E. MacFarlane/Major Harvey A.
   Freehan/Lieutenant Colonel Carl A. Youngdale
4th Battalion, Lieutenant Colonel Carl A. Youngdale/Major Roland J. Spritzen

4th Tank Battalion, Lieutenant Colonel Richard K. Schmidt
4th Engineer Battalion, Lieutenant Colonel Nelson K. Brown
4th Pioneer Battalion, Lieutenant Colonel Richard G. Ruby
4th Service Battalion, Lieutenant Colonel John E. Fondahl
4th Motor Transport Battalion, Lieutenant Colonel Ralph L. Schlesswohl
4th Medical Battalion, Commander Reuben L. Sharp, USNR
5th Amphibian Tractor Battalion, Major George L. Shead
10th Amphibian Tractor Battalion, Major Victor Croizat
1st Joint Assault Signal Company (JASCO)
Marine Observation Squadron 4
7th War Dog Platoon
1st Provisional Rocket Detachment
JICPOA Intelligence Team

5th Division, Major General Keller E. Rockey
26th Regiment, Colonel Chester B. Graham
1st Battalion, Lieutenant Colonel Daniel C. Pollock/Major Albert V. K. Gary
2nd Battalion, Lieutenant Colonel Joseph P. Sayers/Major Amedeo Rea
3rd Battalion, Lieutenant Colonel Tom M. Trotti/Major Richard Fagan

27th Regiment, Colonel Thomas A. Wornham
1st Battalion, Lieutenant Colonel John A. Butler/Lieutenant Colonel Justin G. Duryea/Major William H. Tumbelston/Major William H. Kennedy, Jr.
2nd Battalion, Major John W. Antonelli/Major Gerald F. Russell
3rd Battalion, Lieutenant Colonel Donn J. Robertson

28th Regiment, Colonel Harry B. Liversedge
1st Battalion, Lieutenant Colonel Jackson B. Butterfield
2nd Battalion, Lieutenant Colonel Chandler W. Johnson/Major Thomas B. Pearce, Jr.
3rd Battalion, Lieutenant Colonel Charles E. Shepard, Jr./Major Tolson A. Smoak

13th Regiment [Artillery], Colonel James D. Waller
1st Battalion, Lieutenant Colonel John S. Oldfield
2nd Battalion, Major Carl W. Hjerpe
3rd Battalion, Lieutenant Colonel Henry T. Waller
4th Battalion, Major James F. Coady

Service Troops, Colonel Benjamin W. Gally
5th Tank Battalion, Lieutenant Colonel William R. Collins
5th Engineer Battalion, Lieutenant Colonel Clifford H. Shuey
5th Pioneer Battalion, Major Robert S. Riddell
5th Service Battalion, Major Francis P. Daly/Major Gardelle Lewis
5th Motor Transport Battalion, Major Arthur F. Torgler, Jr.
5th Medical Battalion, Lieutenant Commander William W. Ayres, USNR
3rd Amphibian Tractor Battalion, Lieutenant Colonel Sylvester Stephan
11th Amphibian Tractor Battalion, Lieutenant Colonel Albert J. Roose
5th Joint Assault Signal Company (JASCO)
Marine Observation Squadron 5
6th War Dog Platoon
3rd Provisional Rocket Detachment
JICPOA Intelligence Team
VAC (Major Attached Units)
Corps Troops Commander, Colonel Alton A. Gladden
1st Provisional Field Artillery Group, Colonel John S. Letcher
8th Field Depot, Colonel Leland S. Swindler
Air Support Control Unit, Colonel Vernon E. Megee
Signal Battalion, Lieutenant Colonel Alfred F. Robertshaw
Medical Battalion, Lieutenant Commander William B. Clapp, USNR
Provisional Signal Corps, Lieutenant Colonel Harry W. G. Vadnals

2nd Separate Engineer Battalion, Lieutenant Colonel Charles O. Clark
2nd Armored Amphibian Battalion, Lieutenant Colonel Reed M. Fawell, Jr.
Evacuation Hospital No. 1, Captain H. G. Young, USN
2nd Bomb Disposal Company
Company B, Amphibious Reconnaissance Battalion
Medical Section, Civil Affairs
JICPOA Intelligence Team
JICPOA Enemy Material and Salvage Platoon

## United States Navy

Fifth Fleet, Admiral Raymond A. Spruance (USS *Indianapolis*)
Task Force 51 [Joint Expeditionary Force], Vice Admiral Richmond K. Turner
Task Group 51.1 [Joint Expeditionary Force Reserve], Commodore Donald W. Loomis
Task Group 51.2 [Transport Screen], Captain Frederick Moosbrugger
Task Group 51.3 [Service and Salvage Group], Captain Curtiss
Task Group 51.4 [Hydrographic Survey Group], Commander Sanders
Task Group 51.5-9 [Defense and Garrison Groups]
Task Group 51.10 [Air Support Control Unit]

## Participating Surface Ships

4 command ships
12 aircraft carriers
6 battleships
19 cruisers
44 destroyers
38 destroyer escorts
6 destroyer transports
44 transports
63 LSTs (Landing Ship Tank)
31 LSMs (Landing Ship Medium)
19 cargo ships
6 repair ships
4 seaplane tenders
4 ocean tugs
14 destroyer minecraft
30 minesweepers
5 net layers
76 LCIs (Landing Craft Infantry)

3 LSDs (Landing Ship Dock)

1 LSV (Landing Ship Vehicle)

56 assorted patrol, escort, and support vessels

Task Force 52 [Amphibious Support Force], Rear Admiral William H. P. Blandy

Task Force 53 [Attack Force], Rear Admiral Harry W. Hill

Task Force 54 [Gunfire and Covering Force], Rear Admiral Bertram J. Rodgers

Task Force 56 [Expeditionary Troops], Lieutenant General Holland M. Smith, USMC

Task Group 56.1 [Landing Force], Major General Harry Schmidt

Task Group 56.2 [Assault Troops], 4th Marine Division/Major General Clifton B. Cates, 5th Marine Division/Major General Keller E. Rockey

Task Group 56.3 [Expeditionary Troops Reserve], 3rd Marine Division/Major General Graves B. Erskine

Task Force 58 [Fast Carrier Forces], Vice Admiral Marc A. Mitscher (USS Bunker Hill)

## Task Group 58.1, Rear Admiral Joseph J. Clark

Carriers: *Hornet, Wasp, Bennington, Belleau Wood*
Battleships: *Massachusetts, Indiana*
Cruisers: *Vincennes, Miami, San Juan*
15 destroyers

## Task Group 58.2, Rear Admiral Ralph E. Davison

Carriers: *Lexington, Hancock, San Jacinto*
Battleships: *Wisconsin, Missouri*
Cruisers: *San Francisco, Boston*
19 destroyers

## Task Group 58.3, Rear Admiral Frederick C. Sherman

Carriers: *Essex, Bunker Hill, Cowpens*
Battleships: *South Dakota, New Jersey*
Cruisers: *Alaska, Indianapolis, Pasadena, Wilkes-Barre, Astoria*
14 destroyers

## Task Group 58.4, Rear Admiral Arthur W. Radford

Carriers: *Yorktown, Randolph, Langley, Cabot*
Battleships: *Washington, North Carolina*
Cruisers: *Santa Fe, Biloxi, San Diego*
17 destroyers

## Task Group 58.5
Carriers: *Enterprise*, *Saratoga*
Cruisers: *Baltimore*, *Flint*
12 destroyers

### Seabees
9th Naval Construction Brigade, Captain Robert C. Johnson
41st Naval Construction Regiment [Assault Phase], Commander Paul F. Henderson
31st Battalion [assigned to 5th Marine Division], Lieutenant Commander Dominick J. Ermilio
133rd Battalion [assigned to 4th Marine Division], Lieutenant Commander Ray P. Murphy
62nd Battalion [assigned to VAC], Lieutenant Commander Frank B. Campbell
70th Battalion (half-strength: 15 officers, 285 men, barges, pontoons, causeways)
8th Naval Construction Regiment [Second Phase], Commander Rudolph Y. Taggart
8th Battalion, Commander W. T. Powers
90th Battalion, Commander George S. Brockway
95th Battalion, Commander W.L. Johnson
23rd Battalion [stevedores], Lieutenant Commander H. W. Heuer
301st Battalion [harbor specialists], Commander F. G. Elliot
106th Battalion (Section 2), Lieutenant Commander B. Marcus

### Logistics
Logistic Support Group, Rear Admiral Donald B. Beary
This group was mainly for resupply of Task Force 58 with planes, ammunition, fuel, spare parts, and general supplies. It included:

15 escort carriers
1 cruiser
11 destroyers
18 destroyer escorts
33 tankers
4 ocean tugs
2 ammunition ships
1 general supply ship
Service Squadron 10, Commodore Worrall R. Carter
This squadron of more than 250 ships had headquarters at Ulithi and provided repairs and supplies for all vessels staging through Ulithi, Eniwetok, Guam, and Saipan.

## United States Army

Assault Forces

471st Amphibian Truck Company (attached to 5th Marine Division)

473rd Amphibian Truck Company (attached to VAC), Captain Robert P. Schwabl

476th Amphibian Truck Company (attached to 4th Marine Division), Captain Jules Blaustein

138th Anti-Aircraft Artillery Group, Colonel Clarence E. Rothbeb

Headquarters Battery, 138th AAA

506th AA Gun Battalion, Lieutenant Colonel D. M. White

483rd AAAW Battalion, Lieutenant Colonel A. Roth

38th Field Hospital, Reinforced, Major Samuel S. Kirkland

Detachment, 568th Signal Air Warning Battalion (attached to VAC)

Detachments, 726th Signal Warning Company (attached to VAC, 4th & 5th Marine Divisions)

Detachment, 49th Signal Construction Battalion

Detachment 44, 70th Army Airways Communications Systems

Detachment, Communications Unit 434

442nd Port Company (attached to 4th Marine Division)

592nd Port Company (attached to 5th Marine Division)

Garrison Forces, Major General James E. Chaney

Detachment, Island Command Headquarters

Detachment, 147th Infantry Regiment

Detachment, Headquarters 7th Fighter Command

Detachment, Headquarters 15th Fighter Group

47th Fighter Squadron

78th Fighter Squadron

548th Night Fighter Squadron

386th Air Service Group, Special

1st Platoon, 604th Graves Registration Company

223rd Radar Maintenance Unit, Type C

Port Director Detachment

Garrison Beach Party

# Appendix III

# Weapons: Number, Type and Calibre Used During the Assault on Iwo Jima

| | |
|---|---:|
| (1) Carbine, cal .30 M1 | 32,277 |
| (2) Rifle, Cal .30, M1903 | 109 |
| (3) Rifle, cal .30, M1 | 20,809 |
| (4) Rifle, BAR, cal .30, M1918A2 | 2,630 |
| (5) MG, cal .30, M1917 & M1919 | 2,055 |
| (6) MG Cal .30, M1919A6 | 5 |
| (7) Shotgun, 12 gauge | 624 |
| (8) Pistol, cal .45, M1911 | 2,552 |
| (9) SMG cal .45 | 303 |
| (10) MG, cal .50 M2HB | 941 |
| (11) Gun, 37mm AT M3A1 | 96 |
| (12) Mortar, 60mm | 312 |
| (13) Mortar, 81mm | 102 |
| (14) Gun, 75mm SP, AT or Tk. | 158 |
| (15) Howitzer, 75mm Pack or Amtrac | 123 |
| (16) Howitzer, 105mm | 96 |
| (17) Launcher, 4.5in BR, Mk7 | 61 |
| (18) Launcher, rocket, AT 2.36in | 504 |
| (19) Howitzer, 155mm, M1 | 24 |
| TOTAL | 63,781 |

*Source: Headquarters V Amphibious Corps. Staff Reports. Ordnance*

# Appendix IV

# Casualty Dedication

The text of the sermon that is detailed here was delivered by Rabbi Lieutenant Roland B. Gittelsohn, a US Navy chaplain attached to the US 5th Marine Division, during the dedication service for the 5th Marine Division Cemetery on Iwo Jima, 21 March. Both inspiring and moving, it still resonates today:

No, our poor power of speech can add nothing to what these men and the other dead of our division who are not here have already done. All that we can even hope to do is follow their example. To show the same selfless courage in peace that they did in war. To swear that, by the grace of God and the stubborn strength and power of human will, their sons and ours shall never suffer these pains again.

These men have done their job well. They have paid the ghastly price of freedom. If that freedom be once again lost, as it was after the last war, the unforgivable blame will be ours, not theirs. So, it is the living who are here to be dedicated and consecrated.

We dedicate ourselves, first, to live together in peace the way they fought and are buried in war. Here lie men who loved America because their ancestors, generations ago, helped in her founding, and other men who loved her with equal passion because they themselves or their own fathers escaped from oppression to her blessed shores. Here lie officers and men, Negroes and whites, rich men and poor—together. Here are Protestants, Catholics, and Jews—together. Here no man prefers another because of his faith or despises him because of his color. Here there are no quotas of how many from each group are admitted or allowed. Among these men there is no discrimination. No prejudice. No hatred. Theirs is the highest and purest democracy.

Any man among us, the living, who fails to understand that will thereby betray those who lie here dead. Whoever of us lifts his hand in hate against a brother or thinks himself superior to those who happen to be in the minority, makes of this ceremony and of the bloody sacrifice it commemorates, an empty, hollow mockery. To this, them, as our solemn, sacred duty, do we the living now dedicate ourselves: to the right of Protestants, Catholics and Jews, of white men and Negroes alike, to enjoy the democracy for which all of them have here paid the price.

To one thing more do we consecrate ourselves in memory of those who sleep beneath these crosses and stars. We shall not foolishly suppose, as did the last generation of America's fighting men, that victory on the battlefield will automatically guarantee the triumph of democracy at home. This war, with all its frightful heartache and suffering, is but the beginning of our generation's struggle for democracy. When the last battle has been won, there will be those at home, as there were last time, who will want us to turn our backs in selfish isolation on the rest of organized humanity, and thus to sabotage the very peace for which we fight. We promise you who lie here; we will not do that! We will join hands with Britain, China, Russia—in peace, even as we have in war, to build the kind of world for which you died.

When the last shot has been fired, there will still be those whose eyes are turned backward not forward, who will be satisfied with those wide extremes of poverty and wealth in which the seeds of another war can breed. We promise you, our departed comrades: this, too, we will not permit. This war has been fought by the common man; its fruits of peace must be enjoyed by the common man! We promise, by all that is sacred and holy, that your sons, the sons of miners and millers, the sons of farmers and workers, will inherit from your death the right to a living that is decent and secure.

When the final cross has been placed in the last cemetery, once again there will be those to whom profit is more important than peace, who will insist with the voice of sweet reasonableness and appeasement that it is better to trade with the enemies of mankind than, by crushing them, to lose their profit. To you who sleep here silently, we give our promise: we will not listen! We will not forget that some of you were burnt with oil that came from American wells, that many of you were killed by shells fashioned from American steel. We promise that when once again men seek profit at your expense, we shall remember how you looked when we placed you reverently, lovingly, in the ground.

This do we memorialize those who, having ceased living with us, now live within us. Thus, do we consecrate ourselves, the living, to carry on the struggle they began. Too much blood has gone into this soil for us to let it lie barren. Too much pain and heartache have fertilized the earth on which we stand. We here solemnly swear: this shall not be in vain! Out of this, and from the suffering and sorrow of those who mourn this, will come – we promise – the birth of a new freedom for the sons of men everywhere.

# Appendix V

# Saved by Iwo Jima

A report details of the how the crew of a Boeing B-29 were forced to bale out of their aircraft, but whose lives were saved to the fact that Iwo Jima had been captured by US forces and served as a 'safe haven':

HEADQUARTERS
73rd BOMBARDMENT WING
APO 237, C/O, CSTMASTER
SAN FRANCISCO, CALIFORNIA

373.2 ARCPN                                                                                    1 June 1945
SUBJECT: Emergency Rescue Report #28 (Bailout)

TO: See Distribution

I. BASIC DATA

1.  Mission No.73, 25 May IS45. Date of Report:
2.  Wing: 73. Group 498. Squadron: 875th. A/C Serial Number 42-65211.
3.  Cause of bailout: Engine trouble, Unable to land.
4.  Trouble: Loss of No.1 engine, No.4 engine backfiring severely. Lack of gas to reach home base. Landing field at Iwo Jima completely closed in.
5.  Bailout: 0925K 26 May 1945, over Iwo Jima.
6.  Rescue: All crew members landed on island of Iwo Jima
7.  Crew:

| Position | Name | Rank | ASN | Last Seen |
|----------|------|------|-----|-----------|
| Ap Com | Reeves, John D. | 1st Lt | 0807784 | Rescued |
| Co-pilot | Sullivan, Benj. B. | 2nd Lt | 0831843 | Rescued |
| Navigator | Wagman, Robt. A. | 2nd Lt | 02062719 | Rescued |
| Bombardier | Ingles, John A. | 2nd Lt | 02066177 | Rescued |

| Engineer | Thompson, Russell S. | 2nd Lt | 0869030 | Rescued |
|----------|----------------------|--------|---------|---------|
| Radio Op | Justine, Joseph A. | Cpl | 12239656 | Rescued |
| Radar Op | Dells, Raymond R. | Cpl | 33597101 | Rescued |
| CFC Gnr | Margiotta, Samuel E. | Cpl | 35231228 | Rescued |
| Left Gnr | Skelly, Ralph E. | Cpl | 37606560 | Rescued |
| Right Gnr | Rooman, Richard E. | Cpl | 32993472 | Rescued |
| Tail Gnr | Janasko, Michael | Cpl | 32556407 | Rescued |

8. Interview arranged by Lieutenant Edward J. Tuholske, 489th Bomb Group Personnel Equipment Officer.

## II. NARRATIVE REPORT

1. Development of the emergency: (Narrative by Airplane Commander). On the way to target No.1 engine was leaking a little oil and No.4 engine was backfiring intermittently. I could stop the backfiring on No.4 by changing the power setting and mixture setting. Over the target No.4 backfired very badly and I couldn't keep the recommended power on. After leaving the target the Engineer told me we had forty (40) gallons of oil left in No.1 Engine. The gunners were reporting a Baka right with us, so I had to keep a high-power setting of 38° of Mercury and 2300 RPM. Two hundred miles from the target at an altitude of 19000 feet we encountered bad weather. We feathered No. 1 engine one-half (½) hour before passing Iwo Jima. Iwo Jima was approximately forty (40) miles to our right. We feathered No.1 because by this time the oil was down to fifteen (15) gallons. No.4 engine would backfire severely when attempts were made to carry normal power on it. At the time we feathered No.1 engine the Engineer estimated our gas would run out in four-and-one-half (4½) hours. By this time, we were losing, altitude, two to three hundred (200-300) feet per minute, indicating an airspeed of 170 MPH. I figured that in an hour I would have to apply more power to stay in the air.

The time the Engineer had given me on our gas supply was based on three (3) engine operation; by now we couldn't count on the No.4 engine either. We were about one-hundred (100) miles past Iwo Jima when we decided to turn around and go back to Iwo Jima. I hoped the weather would be clear enough for us to land. As we approached Iwo Jima I called Agate Base on VHF and they advised me to circle the island as they expected the weather to break in in half hour or an hour. The weather at the time was zero zero. I could only see the northwest tip of Iwo Jima and the west side of Mount Suribachi.

The tower told me of another B-29 airplane with four (4) wounded aboard that was trying to land, but had several unsuccessful passes trying to land; this airplane was aided by Ground Control Approach but to no avail. I realised I would have to wait too long until the weather broke. About 0915K (local time) the engineer told me we had 300 gallons of fuel left. We were then at 1500 feet, so I decided to use that gas to climb to give the fellows a hall-decent chance at bailout. I climbed to 3500 feet and made one last circle over the field hoping the weather would break.

I called Agate Base and told them we would have to bailout. They instructed me to fly slightly west of Mount Suribachi on a heading of 50° and bail out, thirty (30) seconds after passing Mount Suribachi. I told my crew members take bailout positions as follows: The left gunner, CFC gunner, right gunner, tail gunner and radar operator by the door in the aft unpressurized section. I had the crew members in the front standing by to bail-out. I circled came in on a heading of 50° and set the C-1 auto pilot as base asked me to be sure that the plane wouldn't crash on the island. The airspeed was about 160-130 MPH.

2. Bail-out: I gave the order bail out (Radar Operator was standing by on interphone) and the five (5) men in the rear bailed out the rear door in the following order: left gunner, right gunner, CFC gunner, tail gunner and radio operator. The navigator went out the front bomb bay followed by the radio operator. The bombardier, engineer, co-pilot and myself in that order bailed out the nose wheel well. All crew members waited five to ten (5-10) seconds before pulling their rip cords.

The descent was uneventful, and no crew member had any difficulty of any kind. Due to the fog no one could see the ground until a split second before hitting. All crew members landed safely on the island. The navigator fractured his left ankle and suffered facial bruises; the left gunner sprained his left foot. No other crew members suffered injury.

# Index